Reading

Follow the arrows to mark the vowels in each word long or short. Then color the arrows according to the code.

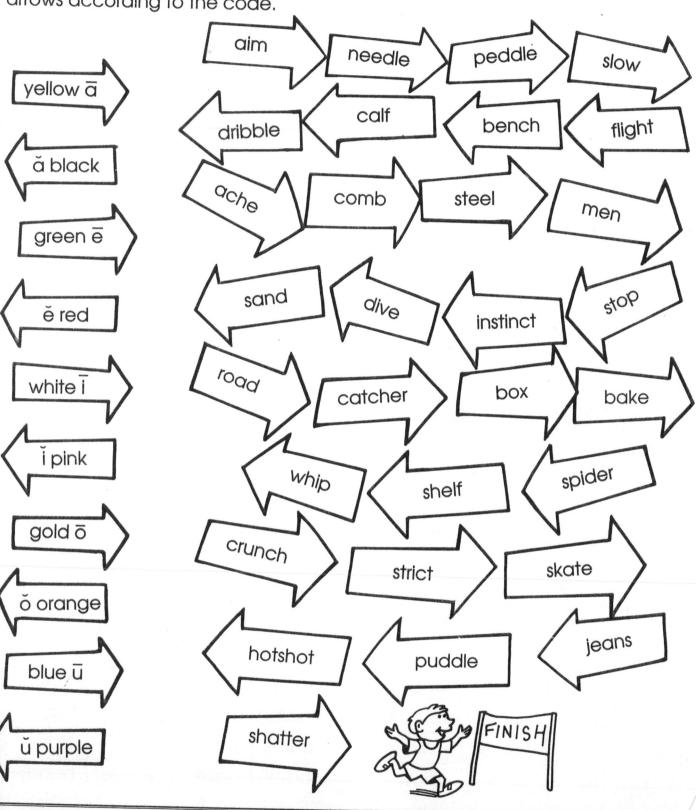

Reading

Name _____

Score four! Find and circle the one row on each grid in which all four words have the same vowel sound. Words can go ↔ ↑ ↗

freight	crab	lamp	man
jump	late	ceiling	cry
lumpy	ill	neigh	stamp
cup	inch	mean	main

honey	blue	funny	sum
pump	two	laugh	clump
flew	chew	sew	dew
crumb	do	under	ump

pets	pencil	letter	type
sight	shred	tight	ride
rip	eyes	review	admit
write	sister	infant	clip

though	fluff	phone	pup
sound	ghost	hut	thought
fudge	stuff	tough	shut
cute	puff	suit	pour

tickle	bride	kids	pickle
write	sit	slime	inch
hiss	into	cries	scribble
pink	stitch	idea	fist

energy	pest	bread	headset
nest	reach	letter	feast
pedal	enemy	red	teach
keep	leather	best	breathe

wove	toast	stove	lobster
bowl	coast	money	popcorn
know	look	broke	cola
ton	roll	only	snow

ramp	ants	lady	act
plate	action	can	shaggy
crank	stamps	slate	paper
back	lake	glasses	handy

IF8786 Fourth Grade in Review

Reading

Name _____

Use the clues to discover the double-letter alphabet words below.
Write each word in the space provided.

AA = _____ African mammal

BB = _____ synonym for hare or bunny

CC = _____ masked animal with ringed tail

DD = _____ not in sight

EE = _____ fastest land animal

FF = _____ bread cooked inside a turkey

GG = _____ where a yellow yolk is found

HH = _____ to thumb a ride

II = _____ sliding down a snowy slope

LL = _____ the home of a hermit crab

MM = _____ a pounding tool

NN = _____ humorous

OO = _____ a chocolate chip treat

PP = _____ large water mammal

RR = _____ feeling bad about something you did

SS = _____ across and down clue-type puzzle

TT = _____ a spacecraft that lands like an airplane

UU = _____ a sweeper

ZZ = _____ light rain

Bonus: Find additional double-letter words for the letters listed.

Reading

Name _____

Read the facts and opinions about Abe Lincoln and George Washington. If the statement is a fact, underline the sentence with blue. If it is an opinion, draw a red circle around the sentence.

1. Washington should not have owned slaves.
2. Abe Lincoln was the best president ever.
3. Lincoln was shot at Ford's Theatre.
4. Mount Vernon was the most beautiful presidential home.
5. Lincoln wrote the Gettysburg Address.
6. Abe felt that slavery was wrong.
7. Washington did not live in the White House.
8. Lincoln was taller than Washington.
9. I think George Washington was a great war general.
10. Abe was tall and skinny.
11. Lincoln was the 16th president of the United States.
12. George Washington was born on a plantation.
13. Some people thought Washington chopped down his father's cherry tree.
14. Abe Lincoln's nickname was "Honest Abe."

Reading

Name _____

The main idea of a paragraph tells what the paragraph is about. Supporting details are sentences that explain the main idea. Write a paragraph for each main idea. Write the main idea first, then write three supporting sentences for each.

Main Ideas

1. Hawaii is a popular tourist site.

2. Computer games can challenge kids' minds.

3. Dolphins are intelligent animals.

1. _____

_____

_____

_____

_____

2. _____

_____

_____

_____

_____

3. _____

_____

_____

_____

_____

Reading

Name _____

Number the baseball action sentences in proper sequence. Then illustrate the third sentence in each group in the matching home plate below.

A.
___ He threw a slider.
___ The pitcher walked to the mound.
___ He went into his wind-up.

C.
___ The batter selected his bat from the bat rack.
___ He rubbed pine tar on the handle
___ He stepped into the batter's box.

B.
___ The ground crew covered the field with the tarp.
___ Dark clouds formed.
___ Heavy rain pelted the ground.

D.
___ It was time for the 7th inning stretch.
___ There were fireworks at the end of the game.
___ "The Star-Spangled Banner" started the game.

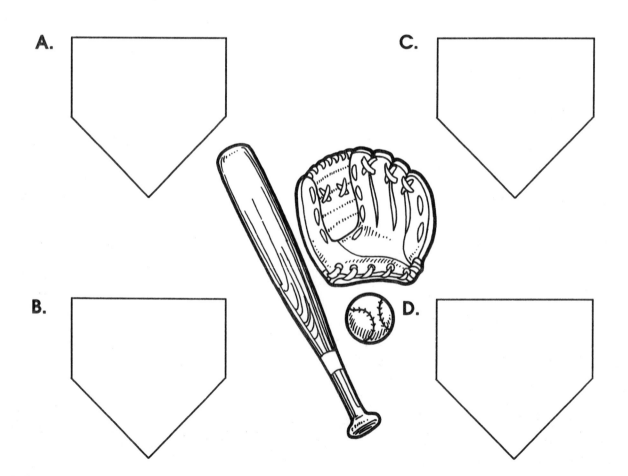

A.

C.

B.

D.

Reading

Name _____

Write each word putting a dot between each syllable.

1. tarantula _____

2. spaniel _____

3. company _____

4. freckle _____

5. violin _____

6. dandelion _____

7. labrador _____

8. sunflower _____

9. alligator _____

10. piccolo _____

11. davenport _____

12. tomorrow _____

13. governor _____

14. numeral _____

15. beginning _____

16. chrysanthemum _____

17. quarrel _____

18. woodpecker _____

19. python _____

20. Eskimo _____

21. potato _____

22. congratulations _____

Reading

Name _____

Invent a new cause to match each effect from the following fairy tales.

1. **Effect:** Old Mother Hubbard went to the cupboard,

    Cause: _____

2. **Effect:** Little Miss Muffet sat on a tuffet,

    Cause: _____

3. **Effect:** Jack and Jill went up the hill,

    Cause: _____

4. **Effect:** Humpty Dumpty sat on a wall,

    Cause: _____

5. **Effect:** Little Bo Peep has lost her sheep,

    Cause: _____

6. **Effect:** Three little kittens they lost their mittens,

    Cause: _____

7. **Effect:** There was an old woman who lived in a shoe,

    Cause: _____

8. **Effect:** Jack Sprat could eat no fat,

    Cause: _____

Reading

Name _____

Add the correct prefix. Then write the new word. In some cases more than one prefix can be used.

in	un	dis	re	im	mis

1. _____ side _____

2. _____ approve _____

3. _____ like _____

4. _____ take _____

5. _____ wind _____

6. _____ patient _____

7. _____ safe _____

8. _____ visible _____

9. _____ connect _____

10. _____ beaten _____

11. _____ believe _____

12. _____ honest _____

13. _____ print _____

14. _____ mature _____

15. _____ write _____

16. _____ proper _____

17. _____ possible _____

18. _____ dependent _____

19. _____ understood _____

20. _____ practical _____

21. _____ cover _____

22. _____ regard _____

Reading

Name _____

Use the Word Bank to fill in the blanks with words containing suffixes. Put each boxed letter in the matching numbered blank below to find the state you migh visit to get something necessary for school.

Word Bank			
invitation	penniless	wonderful	hopeless
careful	noisy	collection	peaceful
addition	followed	winning	

1. h _ □ _ _ _ _ s
2. □ _ d _ t _ _ _
3. _ _ □ _ _ w _ d
4. w _ _ _ □ _ _
5. w _ □ d _ _ _ _ _
6. _ □ r _ f _ _
7. i _ □ _ t _ _ _ _ _
8. c _ _ _ e □ _ _ _ _
9. □ _ i _ y
10. _ _ a _ □ _ _ l
11. _ _ n n □ _ _ _ _

_ _ _ _ _ _ - _ _ _ _ _
1 10 5 8 11 3   7 2 9 4 6

Reading

Name _____

Choose a word from the list on the right to combine with a word on the left to form a compound word.

Example:

_m_	1. chalk	__chalkboard__	a. piece
____	2. over	_____	b. foot
____	3. tooth	_____	c. cycle
____	4. apple	_____	d. mint
____	5. post	_____	e. due
____	6. bare	_____	f. down
____	7. ear	_____	g. spoon
____	8. mouth	_____	h. work
____	9. water	_____	i. sauce
____	10. table	_____	j. melon
____	11. motor	_____	k. right
____	12. wall	_____	l. house
____	13. count	_____	m. board
____	14. light	_____	n. bread
____	15. pepper	_____	o. tub
____	16. basket	_____	p. mark
____	17. ginger	_____	q. ball
____	18. copy	_____	r. ache
____	19. bath	_____	s. paper
____	20. home	_____	t. pick

Reading

Name _____

Find your way through the forest of contractions by writing the contraction in the tree and the letters the apostrophe replaces on the trunk.

Example:

can't

can + not

would + not

were + not

there + is

it + will

let + us

they + will

they + have

who + is

they + would

she + will

does + not

what + is

have + not

here + is

could + not

Reading

Name _____

Write each group of words in alphabetical order. Then write the correct words in the matching spaces at the bottom of the page to find out what Daisy Duck's father said to the shop clerk on the day of Daisy's wedding.

A. opossum   1. _____
  once   2. _____
  on   3. _____
  otter   4. _____

B. put   1. _____
  purse   2. _____
  pump   3. _____
  puddle   4. _____

C. mask   1. _____
  myself   2. _____
  marble   3. _____
  my   4. _____

D. wrong   1. _____
  wrap   2. _____
  wrote   3. _____
  wrist   4. _____

E. issue   1. _____
  it   2. _____
  inch   3. _____
  innocent   4. _____

F. duty   1. _____
  dusty   2. _____
  dump   3. _____
  "ducks-edo"   4. _____

G. bird   1. _____
  binder   2. _____
  biggest   3. _____
  bill   4. _____

H. my   1. _____
  money   2. _____
  most   3. _____
  Mylar   4. _____

I. plead   1. _____
  plea   2. _____
  please   3. _____
  pleasure   4. _____

Answer: _____ _____ _____ _____ and
   I3   D1   H3   F1

_____ _____ _____ _____ _____ .
  B4   E4   A1   C3   G2

Reading

Name _____

Follow the directions.

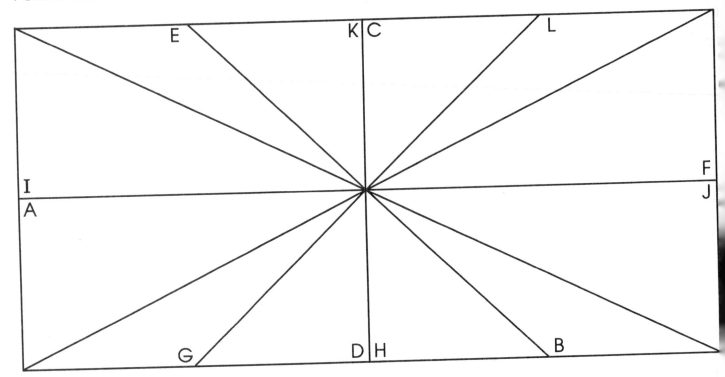

In triangle...

D – draw a green tricycle.

C – draw and color the "Three Blind Mice."

F – write a three-word tongue twister.

I – write three states whose names begin with M.

B – write today's date using only numbers.

E – draw a Triceratops.

L – write the Roman numerals for 3, 30, and 300.

H – write the names of the three summer months.

A – draw George Washington's tricorn hat.

K – write a class motto using three words.

J – draw a spotted cat using three colors.

G – design a pattern using three primary colors.

Reading

Name _____

Write the letter of the alphabet that comes alphabetically after each letter given to identify these famous cartoon characters. Then cut out a speech bubble at the bottom. Match it with the cartoon character who would most likely make that comment.

GNAADR _____	FZQEHDKC _____	CDMMHR the LDMZBD _____
RMNNOX _____	ATFR ATMMX _____	YHFFX _____
RTODQL ZM _____	SVDDSX AHQC _____	LHBJDX LNTRD _____

Meet my buddy, Woodstock.

Watch me get Odie!

I tawt I taw a puddy tat!

I'll change in this phone booth.

Where are you, Calvin?

Mr. Wilson, where are you?

I'm "all ears," Minnie.

What's up, Doc?

Nothing ever goes right for me.

Reading

Name _____

Use the editing marks to correct the book review. Then write the story correctly on another paper.

Editing Marks			
◯ check spelling	ℓ cross out	∧ add	╱ lower case letter
☰ capital letter	♂ move	¶ indent	

twenty seven year old jackie robinson made baseball historie on april 15 1947

he became the first black man to play mager leage baseball in the twentieth

century jackie had to endure numerus insults from those those who felt only

white men should play mager leage baseball but when he was Hired by the

dodgers jackie promised owner branch rickey that would have the guts not to

fite back tho jackie was a man whoo demanded respect he made thot prom-

ise and adhered two it so other black player mite follow in his footsteps today

black baseball players everwhere credit the curage and sacrifices of a grate

Man jackie robinson the first to cross the coler line *

* Jackie Robinson and the Story of All-Black Baseball by Jim O'Connor

Reading

Name _____

Dial these famous pairs.   **Example:** DIAL = 2̇ 3̇ 1̇ 4̇

A B C 1	D E F 2	G H I 3
J K L 4	M N O 5	P Q R 6
S T U 7	V W X 8	Y Z 9

1. 1 1 7 5 1 5   and   6 5 1 3 5   _____

2. 3 1 5 7 2 4   and   3 6 2 7 2 4   _____

3. 4 1 1 4   and   4 3 4 4   _____

4. 6 1 5 5 5 1   and   1 2 2 9 7 7   _____

5. 4 7 1 9   and   2 2 7 3   _____

6. 4 2 6 5 3 7   and   5 3 7 7   6 3 3 3 9   _____

7. 1 2 1 7 7 9   and the   1 2 1 7 7   _____

8. 1 1 4 8 3 5   and   3 5 1 1 2 7   _____

9. 5 3 5 5 3 2   and   5 3 1 4 2 9   5 5 7 7 2   _____

10. 4 1 2 9   and the   7 6 1 5 6   _____

11. 7 5 5 5 6 9   and   1 3 1 6 4 3 2   1 6 5 8 5   _____

12. 3 2 5 6 9   and   6 3 1 7 9   _____

Creative Writing

Name _____

Did you ever wonder what teachers do when they aren't with their students?
Use imagination to write what they might do . . .

on vacation

_____
_____
_____
_____

in their car

_____
_____
_____
_____

at a teacher's meeting

_____
_____
_____
_____

at the grocery store

_____
_____
_____
_____

in their backyard

_____
_____
_____
_____

at a friend's home

_____
_____
_____
_____

at a football game

_____
_____
_____
_____

at a restaurant

_____
_____
_____
_____

 IF8786 Fourth Grade in Review

Creative Writing

Name _____

Your teacher is ill and the principal cannot locate a substitute. You have been asked to take her place for the day. Write your lesson plans.

	Subject	Assignment
7:45 - 8:00	_____	_____
8:00 - 8:30	_____	_____
8:30 - 9:00	_____	_____
9:00 - 9:30	_____	_____
9:30 - 10:30	_____	_____
10:30 - 11:00	_____	_____
11:00 - 11:30	_____	_____
11:30 - 12:30	_____	_____
12:30 - 1:00	_____	_____
1:00 - 1:30	_____	_____
1:30 - 2:00	_____	_____
2:00 - 2:30	_____	_____
2:30 - 3:00	_____	_____

Creative Writing

Name _____

Pretend that your pet could talk. Write what its answer would be to each question.

1. What type of animal are you? _____

2. What is your full name? _____

3. What do you like to be called? _____

4. What is your favorite expression? _____

5. What's your pet peeve? _____

6. What food do you most like to eat? _____

7. What is your favorite game? _____

8. Where do you most like to sleep? _____

9. What is your worst habit? _____

10. What is your favorite animal? _____

11. What is your favorite TV show? _____

12. What is your favorite toy? _____

13. What is your favorite place in the house? _____

14. Why don't you talk in front of anyone else? _____

Creative Writing

Name _____

Your school has an exchange student from ancient Egypt – a mummy! Write about his adventures in your school. Include what can you learn from him.

_____

_____

_____

_____

_____

_____

_____

_____

_____

_____

_____

_____

_____

_____

Design a tomb for the mummy to reside in when you take him back to Egypt.

Creative Writing

Name _____

Did you ever want to give advice to your parents? Well, now is your chance. Write your tips on how to be a perfect parent.

1. _____
_____

2. _____
_____

3. _____
_____

4. _____
_____

5. _____
_____

6. _____
_____

7. _____
_____

8. _____
_____

9. _____
_____

10. _____
_____

Creative Writing

Name _____

Lights! Camera! Action! You are a movie critic. Write a review of your favorite movie. Then illustrate a scene from the beginning, middle, and end of the movie.

Movie Title _____

_____

_____

_____

_____

_____

_____

_____

_____

_____

_____

_____

_____

_____

_____

Beginning	Middle	End

Critical Thinking

Name _____

You have just won $100,000 in the Lucky Lotto. However, to keep the money, you must buy something for each of the following people and animals. Draw what you would give to each.

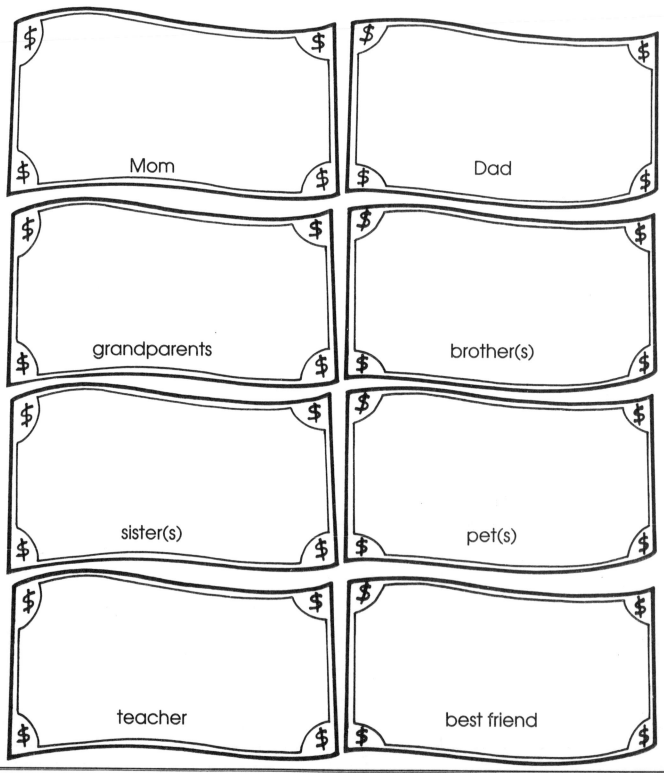

Mom

Dad

grandparents

brother(s)

sister(s)

pet(s)

teacher

best friend

Critical Thinking

Name _____

Let's see how much you know. Answer each question very carefully.

1. Who sits in the chair at the Lincoln Memorial? _____

2. Where was the Korean War fought? _____

3. How many days are in a seven-day week? _____

4. In what city do the Chicago Bulls play? _____

5. What is the product of 9 x 8 x 7 x 6 x 5 x 4 x 3 x 2 x 1 x 0? _____

6. If a plane crashed exactly on the border between the U.S. and Canada, where would the survivors be buried? _____

7. Which state is the Mississippi River named after? _____

8. Which weighs more, a pound of dust or a pound of rocks? _____

9. How do you spell *intelligence*? _____

10. Who wrote the autobiography of Benjamin Franklin? _____

11. Who is buried in Grant's tomb? _____

12. What are JFK's initials? _____

13. How many months have 28 days? _____

14. How long is a four-minute TV commercial? _____

15. How many pennies are in an empty piggy bank? _____

16. How many pickled peppers did Peter Piper pick? _____

17. What fills a helium balloon? _____

18. What color is the White House in Washington, D.C.? _____

English

These sentences make no sense because the words are not in the correct order. Write the sentences correctly beginning with the word that is capitalized and underlined.

1. changed the earth much during <u>The</u> million hundred last years has five

   _____

2. lived 400 fish that ago <u>About</u> had gills both million there years lungs and

   _____

3. forming ago <u>Coral</u> began years 410 reefs million

   _____

4. quickly sail fin the heat Dimetrodon sun's large <u>The</u> collected on the

   _____

5. ago 245 years Age <u>The</u> began million Reptiles about of

   _____

6. reptile word means terrible *dinosaur* <u>The</u>

   _____

7. Brachiosaurus tallest time was the animal of known all <u>The</u>

   _____

8. 150 ago known the years oldest about bird million Archaeopteryx <u>The</u> appeared

   _____

9. vicious Tyrannosaurus a was <u>The</u> dinosaur meat-eating

   _____

10. <u>Scientists</u> extinct not are became dinosaurs sure the why

    _____

11. appeared million plants ago <u>Flowering</u> 138 years

    _____

12. prehistoric are stone in tell <u>Fossils</u> prints us about animals that and plants

    _____

English

Name _____

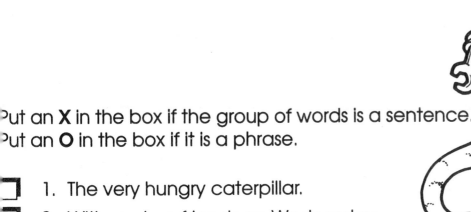

Put an **X** in the box if the group of words is a sentence.
Put an **O** in the box if it is a phrase.

1. The very hungry caterpillar.
2. With my two friends on Wednesday.
3. She overslept.
4. Never had been there before.
5. Three new astronauts were in training.
6. Four barges and one tugboat.
7. Yes, we won our soccer game.
8. A president's term is four years.
9. Her haircut on Tuesday, October 28.
10. Drew, Adam, and Travis.
11. Nicole loved Tweety and Sylvester cartoons.
12. Almost before we got up.
13. I laughed.
14. The robot helped assemble cars.
15. Were on my baseball team.
16. The cobra coiled around its victim.
17. By the time the rescue squad arrived.
18. In the morning newspaper.
19. Vacation begins on June 5.
20. His mom drove a minivan.

© Instructional Fair, Inc.   27   IF8786 Fourth Grade in Review

English

Name _____

Draw a different colored line between the subject and predicate of each sentence

1. You can visit Disney's Magic Kingdom in California or in Florida.
2. The San Diego Zoo is one of our country's best.
3. The Leaning Tower of Pisa in Italy has been leaning for over 600 years!
4. The Space Needle in Seattle, Washington, was built for the 1962 World's Fair.
5. The Statue of Liberty stands on Liberty Island in New York Harbor.
6. The Stone Mountain Memorial near Atlanta, Georgia, honors three famous Southern leaders.
7. Huge statues of Paul Bunyan and Babe the Blue Ox can be seen in Bemidji, Minnesota.
8. Plymouth Rock lies protected in Plymouth, Massachusetts.
9. Mount Vernon, Virginia, was the home of George Washington.
10. The Maid of the Mist is a boat that takes you very close to the bottom of Niagara Falls.
11. The statue of the Great Sphinx in Egypt has the head of a man and the body of a lion.
12. Water collected in the hole of a volcano to form Crater Lake in Oregon.

28   IF8786 Fourth Grade in Review

English

Name _____

Read each sentence. Write **S** for statement, **C** for command, **Q** for question, and **E** for exclamation. Then add the end punctuation mark. Finally, draw the correct design in each box.

| 12. | 9. | 17. | 1. | 6. |

| S red | | | | | 13. |

Example:

_C_ 1. Close that upstairs window.

____ 2. Who is she going to the game with

____ 3. What a colorful rainbow

____ 4. The catsup bottle is empty

____ 5. Whose turn is it on the computer

____ 6. Slide into third base headfirst

____ 7. How did she know your name

____ 8. They won the game in overtime

____ 9. I was too terrified to scream

____ 10. Put your bike in the garage

____ 11. The plane was one hour late

____ 12. Why is your shirt torn

____ 13. Bees pollinate flowers

____ 14. He had a cellular phone in his car

____ 15. Is that your sister

____ 16. What a surprise party

____ 17. Go to the next block and turn left

____ 18. Put your name on your paper

S red

C green

Q blue

E orange

4.

11.

18.

7.

13.

15.

3.

10.

8.

| 2. | 14. | 5. | 16. |

English

Name _____

Choose a synonym from the Word Bank for each word on a Popsicle. Write it on the other half. Then color the half of the Popsicle whose word comes first in alphabetical order.

Word Bank

refuse	occur	shake	choose
purchase	fright	rough	reply
copy	vacant	worth	pledge
genuine	depart	simple	tardy

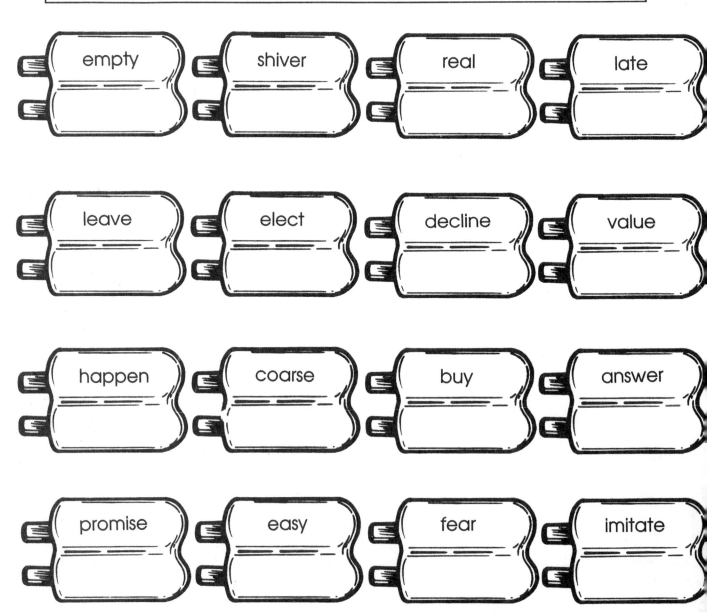

empty shiver real late

leave elect decline value

happen coarse buy answer

promise easy fear imitate

---

30   IF8786 Fourth Grade in Review

English

Name _____

Write the matching antonym for each word.

Word Bank					
innocent	present	interior	victory	doubt	rare
defense	increase	shallow	few	wild	plain
departure	minimum	excited	lazy	smooth	rude

common _____

fancy _____

absent _____

deep _____

many _____

maximum _____

ough _____

polite _____

arrival _____

ambitious _____

decrease _____

offense _____

exterior _____

defeat _____

believe _____

calm _____

guilty _____

tame _____

English

Name _____

Write the correct homonym in the matching room of the Homonym Hotel.

8.		1.	7.	13.	14.
12.	3.	11.	6.		5.
4.	2.	9.		10.	

1. The state of Nevada is mostly (desert, dessert).
2. The family went to Virginia (Beech, Beach).
3. The camper's letter began, (Dear, Deer) Mom and Dad.
4. They visited the (Capital, Capitol) building in Washington, D.C.
5. She (road, rode) the roller coaster four times!
6. (There, Their) minivan had a flat tire.
7. (Meet, Meat) me by the diving board at 3:00.
8. The Lion King sat on his royal (thrown, throne).
9. The elephants at the zoo (paste, paced) back and forth.
10. We (new, knew) our vacation would be in August.
11. Have you ever (bin, been) to New York City.
12. Our dinner was prepared in a Japanese (walk, wok).
13. Our (principle, principal) vacationed in Florida.
14. We toured an old English (manor, manner).

English

Name _____

Use a dictionary to chart the information.

Entry Word	Page #	Guide Words	# of Syllables	# of Meanings	Example Sentence
run					
fair					
can					
play					
bill					
fog					
grade					
press					
flat					
bass					
chip					
cast					
sock					

English

Name _____

Circle the words that would appear between each pair of guide words.

lemon - lilac

lion	least
lunch	letter
little	like

baby - billfold

bank	binder
bill	beast
boa	blister

sandy - soccer

sunshine	seat
sock	silly
saw	socket

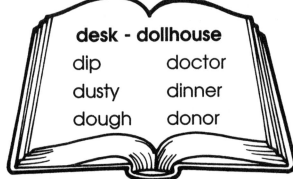

desk - dollhouse

dip	doctor
dusty	dinner
dough	donor

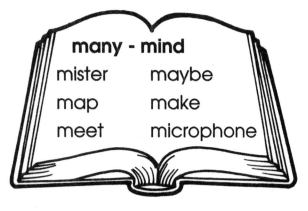

many - mind

mister	maybe
map	make
meet	microphone

tell - tollbooth

test	teacup
today	temper
toad	telephone

clip - cutlery

camera	crush
cup	color
clang	crayon

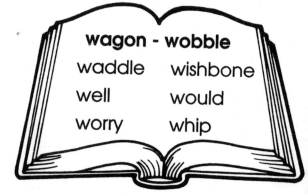

wagon - wobble

waddle	wishbone
well	would
worry	whip

English

Name _____

In which book(s) would you look to find the following information? Mark each sentence according to the key.

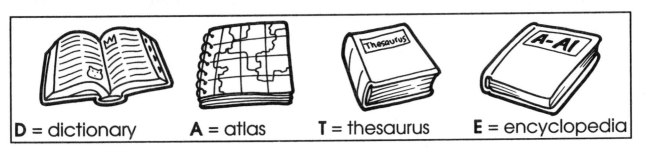

D = dictionary   **A** = atlas   **T** = thesaurus   **E** = encyclopedia

_____ 1. How far is Africa from Asia?

_____ 2. What are synonyms for *good*?

_____ 3. How many meanings does *race* have?

_____ 4. Who was the thirteenth president of the U.S.?

_____ 5. Does the word *monkey* have an example sentence?

_____ 6. Write a report on Antarctica.

_____ 7. How many synonyms are there for *nice*?

_____ 8. Can the word *run* be both a noun and a verb?

_____ 9. What direction does I-75 run in the state of Ohio?

_____ 10. What did the first flag of our country look like?

_____ 11. Could *easy* be a synonym for *simple?*

_____ 12. On which continent is the Amazon River?

_____ 13. Write a report on solar energy.

_____ 14. How many syllables are in the word *tarantula?*

_____ 15. On which continent is India?

English

Name _____

Match the common and proper nouns. Then write your own proper noun after each common noun.

1.	city	___Las Vegas___	_12_	Ramada Inn
2.	car	_____	____	Alexander Graham Be▮
3.	inventor	_____	____	Mountain Dew
4.	president	_____	____	UCLA
5.	football team	_____	____	Mississippi River
6.	college	_____	____	Thanksgiving
7.	restaurant	_____	____	US Air
8.	athletic shoe	_____	____	Garfield
9.	holiday	_____	____	Miami Dolphins
10.	river	_____	____	Patricia Reilly Giff
11.	basketball team	_____	____	Picasso
12.	hotel	_____	____	Orlando
13.	cartoon character	_____	____	Uranus
14.	dog	_____	____	Blue Ridge
15.	airline	_____	____	Nike
16.	soda pop	_____	____	Chicago Bulls
17.	game	_____	____	Honda Accord
18.	author	_____	____	*Sports Illustrated*
19.	magazine	_____	____	Neil Armstrong
20.	artist	_____	____	John F. Kennedy
21.	astronaut	_____	____	Stegosaurus
22.	planet	_____	____	German shepherd
23.	dinosaur	_____	____	Nintendo
24.	mountain range	_____	____	Burger King

IF8786 Fourth Grade in Revie▮

English

Name _____

Write the plural of each noun below. Then draw a box around each plural using the correct color to show the plural rule followed.

Red add s	Blue change y to i and add es	Orange f to v and add es	Brown irregular word change	Green add es if word ends in s, x, z, ch, or sh

watch _____

lily _____

sandwich _____

man _____

crayon _____

church _____

bunny _____

mouse _____

woman _____

box _____

wolf _____

monster _____

calf _____

school _____

elf _____

child _____

foot _____

shelf _____

lady _____

table _____

tooth _____

daisy _____

English

Name _____

In each football, write a pronoun that could take the place of the underlined words.

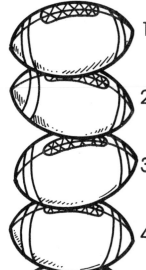

1. Football developed from soccer, although football players may throw the football or carry <u>the football</u>.

2. Lou Holtz's players at Notre Dame respect <u>Lou Holtz</u>.

3. <u>Chad and my</u> team won our division title.

4. The quarterback could pass the ball to <u>Brad and me</u>, since we were receivers.

5. The Michigan Wolverines won the Big Ten, <u>Michigan's</u> conference.

6. <u>The tackles</u> practiced and drilled four hours each day.

7. The coach sent in a play that the quarterback sent back to <u>the coach</u>.

8. The player's shoulder pads slipped off <u>the player's</u> shoulders.

9. The game was tied, so <u>the game</u> went into overtime.

10. The football officials met to discuss a decision one of <u>the officials</u> had made.

11. If a player commits a penalty, <u>the player's</u> team is penalized by the loss of yards or a down.

English

Name _____

or each picture, write two verbs to show actions the object could perform.

_____ _____ _____ _____

_____ _____ _____ _____

_____ _____ _____ _____

In each box below, draw an object that could do the two actions listed.

 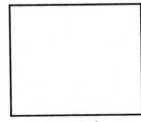 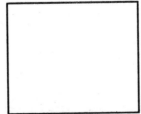 

play   croak   inflate   gobble
record   hop   pop   strut

39   IF8786 Fourth Grade in Review

English

Name _____

Write two lines of conversation between the two characters given. Use quotation marks.

1. Garfield and Odie

   A. _____

   B. _____

2. Charlie Brown and Lucy

   A. _____

   B. _____

3. Dennis the Menace and Mr. Wilson

   A. _____

   B. _____

4. Aladdin and his genie

   A. _____

   B. _____

5. Batman and Robin

   A. _____

   B. _____

6. Superman and Lois Lane

   A. _____

   B. _____

7. Fred Flintstone and Barney Rubble

   A. _____

   B. _____

8. Kermit and Miss Piggy

   A. _____

   B. _____

English

Name _____

Write an example for each rule of capitalization.

Use capital letters on . . .

1. abbreviations _____

2. addresses _____

3. book titles _____

4. calendars _____

5. dates _____

6. the first word of a sentence _____

7. the first word of a quotation _____

8. friendly letters _____

9. initials _____

10. people's names _____

11. cities _____

12. companies _____

13. states _____

14. countries _____

15. a pronoun _____

16. stores _____

17. holidays _____

18. restaurants _____

19. cars _____

20. pet names _____

21. oceans _____

22. team names _____

English

Name _____

Write the abbreviation on the short crayon.

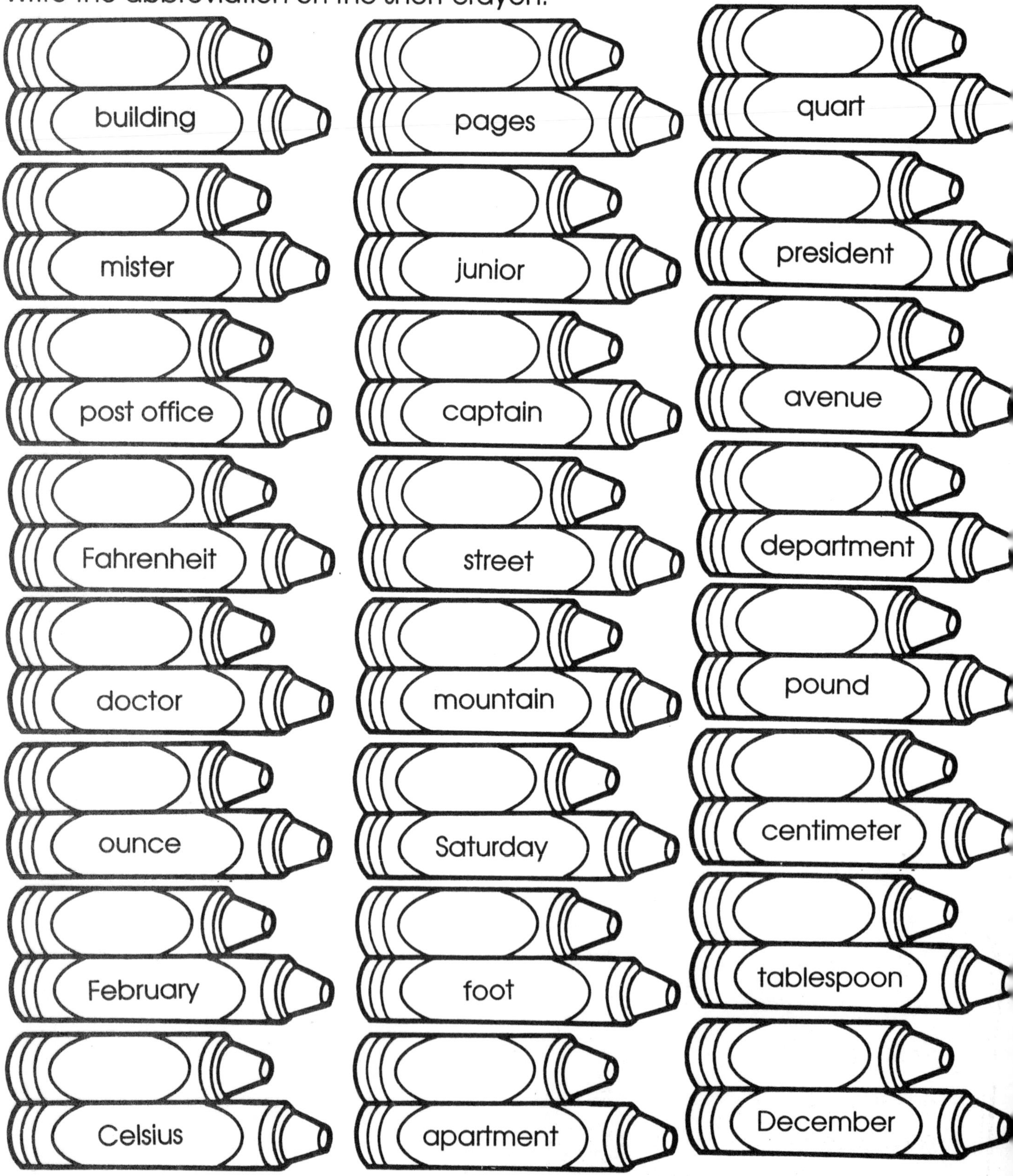

building

pages

quart

mister

junior

president

post office

captain

avenue

Fahrenheit

street

department

doctor

mountain

pound

ounce

Saturday

centimeter

February

foot

tablespoon

Celsius

apartment

December

English

Name ______________________

Write a friendly letter to your best friend describing the best summer vacation you ever had (real or imaginary). Then box each letter part in the color given in the mailbox.

____

____

____

Dear ________________,

____

____

____

____

____

____

____

____

____

____

____

____

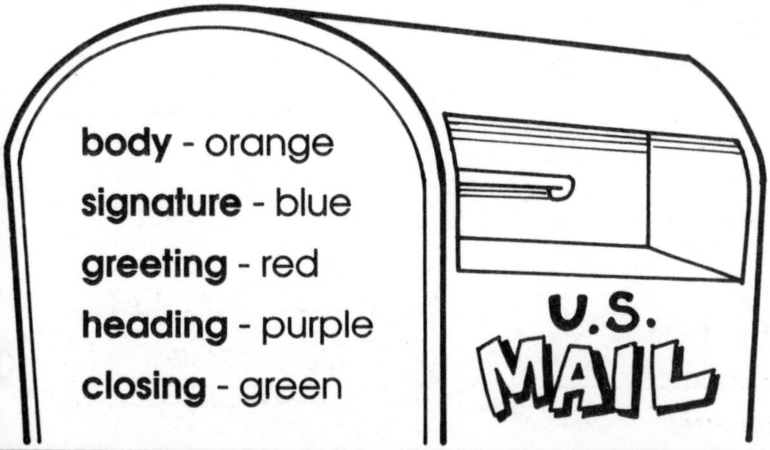
body - orange
signature - blue
greeting - red
heading - purple
closing - green
U.S.
MAIL

________________,

____

English

Name _____

Write an adjective on each side of the triangle to describe the noun inside it.

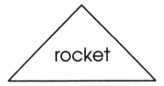 rocket

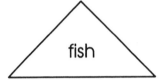 fish

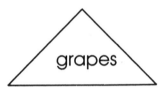 grapes

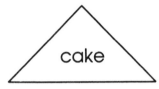 cake

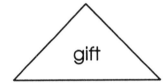 gift

 baby

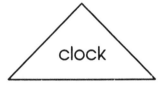 clock

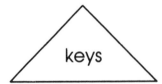 keys

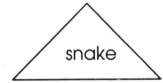 snake

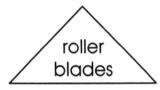 roller blades

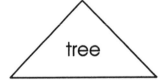 tree

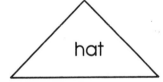 hat

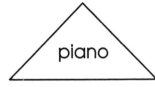 piano

 hair

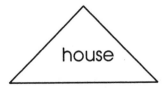 house

English

Name _____

Complete each sentence by writing an adverb that tells how, where, or when.

1. The baseball whizzed _____ past the batter.

(how)

2. The crowd cheered _____ .

(how)

3. The shortstop threw _____ to first base.

(how)

4. The players left their hotel _____ .

(when)

5. The American Airlines jet arrived _____ .

(when)

6. The Toronto Blue Jays traveled _____ .

(where)

7. Several opposing players wandered into the clubhouse _____ .

(when)

8. The outfielder ran _____ than the catcher.

(how)

9. The team practiced _____ because of the rain.

(where)

10. The umpire made the tough call _____ .

(how)

11. The team's manager argued the call _____ .

(how)

12. The rookie never batted _____ .

(how)

13. The stadium was built _____ .

(when)

14. Many of the fans departed _____ at the end of the ninth inning.

(how)

15. The catcher threw the runner out _____ .

(how)

16. Baseball players exercise _____ .

(when)

17. We looked _____ when the ball was hit.

(where)

18. The pitcher threw the ball _____ .

(where)

English

Name _____

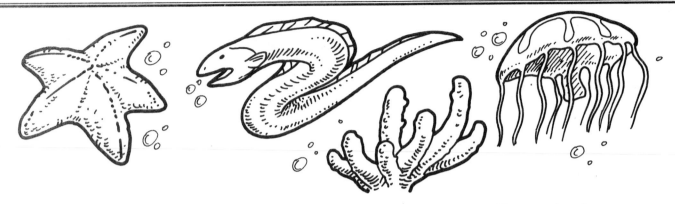

In each sentence, box the parts of speech according to the color key.

Noun - red	Pronoun - yellow	Adjective - green	Adverb - orange	Verb - blue

1. Although they are sea animals, sea anemones, corals, and sponges look more like plants.

2. The eel resembles a snake, but it is really a fish.

3. Whales and dolphins need to put their heads above water and breathe air.

4. Most fish breathe with gills.

5. A squid has a shell that grows inside its body.

6. An oyster has two shells joined by a hinge.

7. A starfish's points are its arms, which can regenerate if lost.

8. Most starfish have five arms, but some can have as many as fifty.

9. Plankton are tiny, microscopic plants and animals that float freely in the ocean.

10. Blue whales grow majestically and can be as long as a row of eight elephants.

11. A jellyfish has no bones and is shaped like an umbrella.

Math

Name _____

Use the code to write a number in each shape. Then add to find the answer.

Example: $\boxed{1}$ + $\boxed{3}$ = $\underline{4}$

1. ⌴ + ⌐ = _____

2. ⌐ + ⌐ = _____

3. ∟ + ⌐ = _____

4. ⌐ + ⌐ = _____

5. ⌴ + ⊓ = _____

6. ⌐ + ⌐ = _____

7. ⌴ + ⌴ = _____

8. ⌐ + ∟ = _____

9. ⌴ + ∟ = _____

10. ⊓ + ⊓ = _____

11. ∟ + ∟ = _____

12. ⊏ + □ = _____

13. ⌐ + ⌐ = _____

14. ∟ + ⌐ = _____

15. ⌐ + ⌐ = _____

16. ⌐ + ⌐ = _____

17. ∟ + ⊏ = _____

18. ⌐ + ⌴ = _____

19. ⊓ + ⊏ = _____

20. ∟ + ⌐ = _____

21. ⊏ + ⌐ = _____

22. ⌐ + ⌴ = _____

23. ⊓ + ∟ = _____

24. ⌐ + ⊓ = _____

25. ⌐ + ⌴ = _____

26. ⌴ + ⌴ = _____

27. ⌐ + □ = _____

28. ⌴ + ⊏ = _____

29. ⌐ + ⊓ = _____

30. ⌐ + ⊏ = _____

Math

Name _____

Write each problem using the code. Then find each answer.

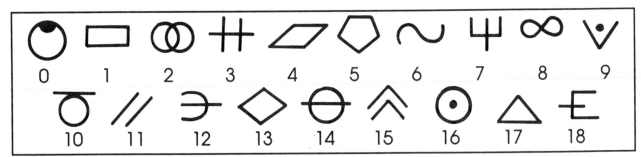

	0		1		2		3		4		5		6		7		8		9

| 10 | 11 | 12 | 13 | 14 | 15 | 16 | 17 | 18 |

$$\odot = \_\_$$
$$-\infty = \_\_$$

$$// = \_\_$$
$$-\Psi = \_\_$$

$$\diamondsuit = \_\_$$
$$-\pentagon = \_\_$$

$$\ni = \_\_$$
$$-\vee = \_\_$$

$$\triangle = \_\_$$
$$-\vee = \_\_$$

$$\ominus = \_\_$$
$$-\infty = \_\_$$

$$\overline{O} = \_\_$$
$$-\oplus = \_\_$$

$$\gg = \_\_$$
$$-\vee = \_\_$$

$$\mathsf{E} = \_\_$$
$$-\vee = \_\_$$

$$\gg = \_\_$$
$$-\infty = \_\_$$

$$\odot = \_\_$$
$$-\Psi = \_\_$$

$$\ni = \_\_$$
$$-\sim = \_\_$$

$$\ominus = \_\_$$
$$-\Psi = \_\_$$

$$\diamondsuit = \_\_$$
$$-\square\!\!\!\!/ = \_\_$$

$$\triangle = \_\_$$
$$-\infty = \_\_$$

$$// = \_\_$$
$$-\sim = \_\_$$

$$\diamondsuit = \_\_$$
$$-\infty = \_\_$$

$$\ni\!\!\!\Psi = \_\_$$
$$-\Psi = \_\_$$

$$\gg = \_\_$$
$$-\sim = \_\_$$

$$\mathsf{E}\overline{O} = \_\_$$
$$- = \_\_$$

$$\gg = \_\_$$
$$-\Psi = \_\_$$

$$// = \_\_$$
$$-\oplus = \_\_$$

$$\ominus = \_\_$$
$$-\vee = \_\_$$

$$\odot = \_\_$$
$$-\vee = \_\_$$

$$\mathsf{E} = \_\_$$
$$-\mathsf{E} = \_\_$$

$$\triangle = \_\_$$
$$-\odot = \_\_$$

$$\sim = \_\_$$
$$-\square\!\!\!\!/ = \_\_$$

$$\oplus = \_\_$$
$$-\oplus = \_\_$$

Math

Name _____

Finish each number pattern by writing the next three numbers in the pattern.
Then give the rule the pattern follows.

Rule

1. 7, 14, 21, 28, _____ , _____ , _____   _____

2. 89, 98, 90, 97, _____ , _____ , _____   _____

3. 1, 1, 2, 3, _____ , _____ , _____   _____

4. 2, 6, 12, 20, _____ , _____ , _____   _____

5. 40, 36, 32, 28, _____ , _____ , _____   _____

6. 2, 4, 8, 16, _____ , _____ , _____   _____

7. 1, 20, 300, 4000, _____ , _____ , _____   _____

8. 98, 97, 95, 92, _____ , _____ , _____   _____

9. 72, 60, 48, 36, _____ , _____ , _____   _____

10. 81, 90, 99, 108, _____ , _____ , _____   _____

11. 1, 3, 7, 15, _____ , _____ , _____   _____

12. 1, 5, 25, 125, _____ , _____ , _____   _____

Math

Name _____

Show the place value of each underlined digit by outlining each placemat according to the color code.

ones - purple **tens** - green **hundreds** - orange	**one thousands** - red **ten thousands** - yellow **hundred thousands** - blue	**one millions** - pink **ten millions** - brown **hundred millions** - black

456,7<u>4</u>2

9,03<u>2</u>

<u>7</u>2,467

<u>9</u>00,406

501,3<u>3</u>7

12,<u>4</u>78,922

7<u>8</u>9,604,311

5,<u>6</u>94

11<u>2</u>,789,421

973,<u>5</u>61

4,729,00<u>2</u>

<u>3</u>25,846

4<u>3</u>9,012,115

5,6<u>7</u>3,214

<u>6</u>09,184

2,117,<u>4</u>98

817,3<u>6</u>4

<u>8</u>9,645

5,<u>3</u>73,417

77,004,06<u>7</u>

<u>1</u>,592,377

<u>2</u>43,169,050

9,371,<u>5</u>92

<u>9</u>39,044

<u>2</u>0,188,953

13,<u>6</u>59,171

<u>8</u>8,904

7,<u>6</u>14,252

25,<u>2</u>01,814

2,067,<u>7</u>46

90,385,4<u>2</u>7

3,527,<u>8</u>16

Math

Name _____

| I = 1 | V = 5 | X = 10 | L = 50 | C = 100 | D = 500 | M = 1,000 |

Examples: IV = 4, V = 5, VI = 6

Write the Roman numerals for . . .

17 _____	115 _____	1846 _____
39 _____	309 _____	1901 _____
55 _____	510 _____	1562 _____
83 _____	972 _____	1492 _____
76 _____	414 _____	1001 _____
3 _____	96 _____	1776 _____
89 _____	338 _____	1295 _____

Write the standard numerals for . . .

VII _____	CCI _____	MCMLXXXI _____
XIX _____	DCLXXIII _____	MCDXXII _____
XLI _____	CDV _____	MCMXLV _____
LXXVIII _____	CLIII _____	MCMXCIV _____
XXXII _____	DCCIV _____	CMXLVII _____
LXVI _____	DXXXII _____	CCCLXVI _____
XVII _____	CDVIII _____	MCMII _____
LI _____	DCLXVI _____	MCCCXV _____

Math

Name _____

Go through the maze by adding each number to the answer from the previous box.

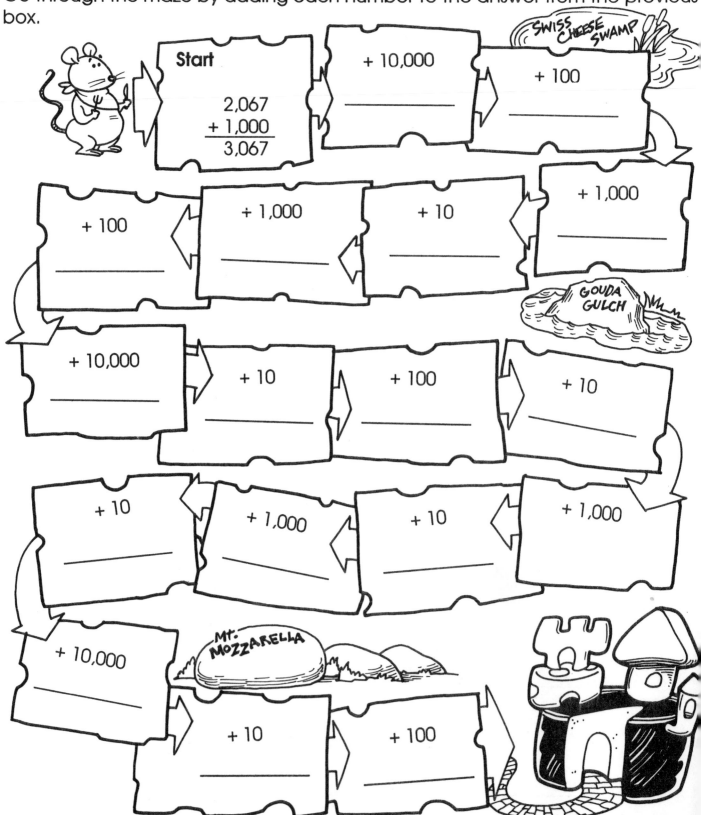

Start

2,067
+ 1,000
———
3,067

+ 10,000

SWISS CHEESE SWAMP

+ 100

+ 100

+ 1,000

+ 10

+ 1,000

GOUDA GULCH

+ 10,000

+ 10

+ 100

+ 10

+ 10

+ 1,000

+ 10

+ 1,000

+ 10,000

Mt. MOZZARELLA

+ 10

+ 100

Name _____

Put an **X** on the box with the sign which should be used when comparing the pair of numbers. Write the letter from the X'd box on the matching numbered lines below to answer the riddle.

1.	164,982	N <	> F	164,892
2.	27,493,171	C <	> A	27,493,717
3.	13,562,439	R <	> S	13,562,349
4.	60,871,956	M <	> T	60,871,695
5.	34,742	C <	> A	34,472
6.	19,584,578	D <	> K	19,584,785
7.	746,361,294	N <	> L	746,361,492
8.	600,100,001	B <	> Y	600,010,001
9.	88,914,676	N <	> T	88,914,767
10.	41,200,050	Y <	> O	41,200,500
11.	841,762,145	D <	> R	841,762,514
12.	27,181,426	N <	> I	27,181,246
13.	38,226,943	P <	> K	38,226,349
14.	80,000,001	O <	> I	80,000,010
15.	500,146,271	S <	> U	500,146,172
16.	15,836,504	N <	> F	15,836,054
17.	20,673,746	R <	> I	20,673,476

What do ducks call word meanings in their dictionaries?

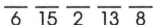

‾6‾ ‾15‾ ‾2‾ ‾13‾ ‾8‾   ‾11‾ ‾5‾ ‾16‾ ‾1‾ ‾10‾ ‾7‾ ‾12‾ ‾4‾ ‾17‾ ‾14‾ ‾9‾ ‾3‾

Math

Name _____

Work each problem. Then write each letter on the matching numbered line to answer the riddle below.

Ⓞ
1. 986
   459
  +277

Ⓞ
2. 7,466
   9,572
  +8,666

Ⓔ
3. 98,462
  15,361
  +48,795

Ⓐ
4. 77,313
  19,458
  +83,919

Ⓢ
5. 8,335
   7,868
  +1,344

Ⓔ
6. 80,476
  12,552
  +37,818

Ⓘ
7. 989
   245
  +777

Ⓗ
8. 54,942
  17,157
  +30,062

Ⓡ
9. 421
   667
  +819

Ⓛ
10. 16,490
  32,527
  +47,162

Ⓡ
11. 9,155
   6,989
  +2,416

Ⓞ
12. 22,705
  18,594
  +66,080

Ⓣ
13. 914
   266
  +888

Ⓣ
14. 17,496
  20,357
  +19,042

Ⓔ
15. 696
   247
  +358

Ⓜ
16. 1,466
   8,754
  +3,083

Ⓑ
17. 24,716
  54,850
  +66,274

What American League baseball team goes best with milk?

$\overline{13}$ $\overline{8}$ $\overline{3}$ $\overline{17}$ $\overline{4}$ $\overline{10}$ $\overline{14}$ $\overline{7}$ $\overline{16}$ $\overline{1}$ $\overline{11}$ $\overline{6}$ $\overline{2}$ $\overline{9}$ $\overline{15}$ $\overline{12}$ $\overline{5}$

Math

Name _____

Work each problem. If the answer is on a Bingo card, color the square. Draw a line through the winning row.

600 − 156	2,146 − 1,098	883 − 455	6,114 − 3,762	8,492 − 7,588
411 − 77	5,005 − 3,119	708 − 499	4,593 − 1,774	3,051 − 1,662
500 − 174	9,384 − 5,745	413 − 153	2,001 − 966	4,972 − 2,674
624 − 335	7,051 − 3,223	904 − 713	5,275 − 1,699	3,231 − 869
971 − 652	5,047 − 2,736	812 − 525	6,711 − 4,472	4,000 − 2,096

B	I	N	G	O
1,886	147	289	502	904
1,389	287	616	1,035	841
2,311	303	3,639	1,162	428
4,004	1,904	311	3,640	913
2,352	405	2,362	2,067	2,298

B	I	N	G	O
444	520	209	1,664	2,239
343	1,814	907	1,048	326
3,576	334	1,776	2,750	3,828
1,907	191	288	260	2,365
3,575	460	2,819	2,238	319

Math

Name _____

Work each problem. Then lightly color the boxes blue whose answers have an "8" in them. This path should lead you to the island.

746 +292	597 +366	943 +769	848 +888	357 +867	677 +788
499 +799	385 +496	447 +691	595 +377	201 +489	143 +798
355 +299	814 +296	249 +936	932 +384	359 +367	484 +947
649 +497	390 +956	479 +369	526 +577	254 +996	394 +777
751 +179	947 +265	542 +939	963 +872	307 +469	486 +293
875 +146	436 +296	265 +171	596 +274	371 +639	563 +199
195 +279	957 +285	167 +448	194 +588		

Addend
Island

56   IF8786 Fourth Grade in Review

Math

Name _____

Work each problem. Then write each letter on the matching numbered line to answer the riddle below.

Ⓝ
1. 400
  − 267

Ⓞ
2. 311
  − 89

Ⓟ
3. 825
  − 359

Ⓐ
4. 603
  − 358

Ⓝ
5. 912
  − 475

Ⓐ
6. 924
  − 599

Ⓚ
7. 722
  − 344

Ⓡ
8. 517
  − 268

Ⓣ
9. 812
  − 435

Ⓒ
10. 201
  − 77

Ⓘ
11. 662
  − 173

Ⓐ
12. 804
  − 139

Ⓘ
13. 743
  − 298

Ⓝ
14. 310
  − 167

What do you call a country in which all of the cars are pink?

$\dfrac{}{6}$ $\dfrac{}{3}$ $\dfrac{}{11}$ $\dfrac{}{14}$ $\dfrac{}{7}$ - $\dfrac{}{10}$ $\dfrac{}{4}$ $\dfrac{}{8}$ $\dfrac{}{1}$ $\dfrac{}{12}$ $\dfrac{}{9}$ $\dfrac{}{13}$ $\dfrac{}{2}$ $\dfrac{}{5}$

Math

Name _____

Watch the signs as you add and subtract these money problems.

$31.16
−17.47

$84.12
+ 16.69

$40.07
− 26.49

$57.45
+ 29.36

$73.21
−46.09

$53.29
+ 77.18

$64.47
−19.56

$81.51
+ 37.88

$20.00
− 6.43

$37.14
+ 18.49

$30.05
− 9.98

$57.69
+ 34.78

$10.11
− 5.16

$86.55
+ 24.93

$41.23
− 27.88

$25.95
+ 37.78

$30.00
− 6.46

$71.86
+ 68.95

$20.67
− 4.98

$39.99
+ 96.77

$11.14
− 6.35

$56.49
+ 54.77

$50.00
− 39.77

$57.66
+19.48

IF8786 Fourth Grade in Review

Math

Name _____

Tell whose face appears on the front of each U.S. coin and bill.

 _____

 _____

 _____

 _____

 _____

$1	🙂	$1
$5	🙂	$5
$10	🙂	$10
$20	🙂	$20
$50	🙂	$50
$100	🙂	$100
$500	🙂	$500
$1000	🙂	$1000

_____

_____

_____

_____

_____

_____

_____

Math

Name _____

Draw the coins and/or bills you might receive as change in each situation.

You have . . .	Your purchase costs . . .	Your change is . . .
1. $10.00	$4.68	
2. $10.00	$6.98	
3. $15.00	$13.97	
4. $20.00	$10.45	
5. $25.00	$23.97	
6. $10.00	$5.67	
7. $5.00	$1.99	
8. $20.00	$14.62	
9. $3.00	$2.18	
10. $10.00	$5.91	

Math

Name _____

Give the time to the exact minute.

_____ _____ _____ _____ _____

_____ _____ _____ _____ _____

_____ _____ _____ _____ _____

_____ _____ _____ _____ _____

IF8786 Fourth Grade in Review

Math

Name _____

Prince Pepperoni is busy baking at his Pizza Palace. Help him complete his baking schedule. The first one is done for you.

In the Oven	Baking Time	Out of the Oven
5:00	20 minutes	5:20
7:45	1½ hours	
8:17		8:52
6:53	45 minutes	
3:11	1 hour 15 minutes	
7:12		8:00
3:47	25 minutes	
9:08		9:54
10:05	1 hour 10 minutes	
4:44		5:09
11:28	35 minutes	

Math

Name _____

Below each box write a word using the numerical prefixes given. Then illustrate each word.

uni = 1 _____

bi = 2 _____

tri = 3 _____

quad = 4 _____

penta = 5 _____

kilo = 1000 _____

octo = 8 _____

deca = 10 _____

Math

Name _____

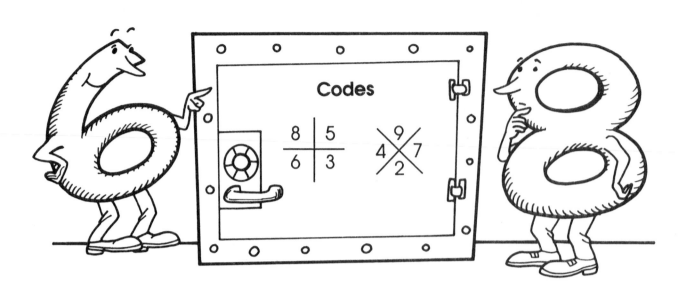

Codes

$$\frac{8}{6} \,\bigg|\, \frac{5}{3} \qquad \overset{9}{\underset{2}{4\!\times\!7}}$$

Write the equation and product for each coded problem.

Example:

└ x ∧ = __10__

(5 x 2 = 10)

⌐ x ⟨ = ___	└ x └ = ___	⌐ x ∧ = ___
∨ x ⌐ = ___	⟩ x ⌐ = ___	∨ x ⟩ = ___
⟨ x └ = ___	⟨ x ⟨ = ___	⌐ x ⌐ = ___
∨ x ∨ = ___	└ x ⌐ = ___	⟨ x ⟩ = ___
⌐ x ∨ = ___	⌐ x ⌐ = ___	∧ x ⟨ = ___
└ x ⌐ = ___	⌐ x ⌐ = ___	⟩ x └ = ___
⌐ x ⟨ = ___	⌐ x ⌐ = ___	└ x ⌐ = ___
⌐ x ⌐ = ___	∨ x └ = ___	⟩ x ⟩ = ___
⌐ x ⟩ = ___	⟨ x ⌐ = ___	⌐ x ⟩ = ___

Math

Name _____

Write each missing number.

$24 \div 8 =$ _____ $16 \div$ _____ $= 4$ $12 \div 2 =$ _____   _____ $\div 6 = 6$

$42 \div$ _____ $= 7$ _____ $\div 4 = 8$ $18 \div 9 =$ _____ $20 \div$ _____ $= 4$

_____ $\div 9 = 8$ $12 \div 3 =$ _____ $64 \div$ _____ $= 8$ $9 \div 3 =$ _____

$49 \div$ _____ $= 7$ _____ $\div 5 = 7$ $48 \div$ _____ $= 6$ $7 \div$ _____ $= 7$

$30 \div 5 =$ _____   _____ $\div 5 = 8$ _____ $\div 2 = 8$ $24 \div 6 =$ _____

_____ $\div 9 = 9$ $54 \div$ _____ $= 6$ $18 \div 6 =$ _____   _____ $\div 7 = 3$

$27 \div 9 =$ _____ $28 \div$ _____ $= 7$ $56 \div 7 =$ _____ $3 \div$ _____ $= 3$

_____ $\div 8 = 6$ $8 \div$ _____ $= 2$ _____ $\div 5 = 2$ _____ $\div 5 = 5$

$36 \div$ _____ $= 6$ $40 \div 5 =$ _____ $72 \div$ _____ $= 9$ $12 \div$ _____ $= 3$

$14 \div 7 =$ _____   _____ $\div 7 = 7$ _____ $\div 3 = 3$ $35 \div 7 =$ _____

_____ $\div 4 = 4$ $32 \div$ _____ $= 4$ $9 \div$ _____ $= 9$ _____ $\div 8 = 8$

Math

Name _____

Solve each problem.

$5\overline{)18}$ $6\overline{)34}$ $8\overline{)70}$ $8\overline{)42}$

$9\overline{)55}$ $5\overline{)43}$ $2\overline{)19}$ $9\overline{)65}$

$7\overline{)48}$ $3\overline{)29}$ $7\overline{)40}$ $4\overline{)30}$

$6\overline{)46}$ $9\overline{)20}$ $6\overline{)58}$ $8\overline{)36}$

$4\overline{)15}$ $3\overline{)16}$ $8\overline{)21}$ $7\overline{)24}$

$2\overline{)9}$ $5\overline{)48}$ $4\overline{)34}$ $9\overline{)50}$

$3\overline{)20}$ $9\overline{)38}$ $7\overline{)18}$ $6\overline{)43}$

$9\overline{)49}$ $2\overline{)17}$ $6\overline{)28}$ $3\overline{)11}$

Math

Name _____

Work a problem on your calculator. Write the answer. Then turn your calculator upside down and write the word to match each clue.

	Answer	Clue	Word
1. $10,252 - 2,538 =$	_____	Raised land	_____
2. $1,777 \times 4 =$	_____	To heat water until it bubbles	_____
3. $2,864 + 2,799 =$	_____	Go well with bacon	_____
4. $253,867 \times 2 =$	_____	Salutations	_____
5. $114,891 - 57,175$	_____	Fish breathe through these	_____
6. $23,573 + 31,503 =$	_____	A shiny finish	_____
7. $1,401 \times 4 =$	_____	Big eaters	_____
8. $11,543 \times 5 =$	_____	Window ledges	_____
9. $26,589 + 26,456 =$	_____	Sock "mates"	_____
10. $104,660 - 53,945 =$	_____	Found on farms	_____
11. $94,154 \times 4$	_____	Laugh	_____

Math

Name _____

Find the product of each problem.

1. | 58 | 34 | 66 | 79 | 84 | 92 |
    | x 6 | x 9 | x 4 | x 3 | x 7 | x 7 |

2. | 17 | 69 | 38 | 64 | 29 | 86 |
    | x 5 | x 8 | x 7 | x 6 | x 6 | x 7 |

3. | 317 | 293 | 835 | 196 | 242 | 588 |
    | x 5 | x 8 | x 7 | x 3 | x 7 | x 4 |

4. | 625 | 434 | 927 | 842 | 364 | 619 |
    | x 8 | x 9 | x 7 | x 8 | x 3 | x 5 |

5. | 4,172 | 3,864 | 8,060 | 1,577 | 9,937 |
    | x 7 | x 6 | x 6 | x 4 | x 9 |

6. | 1,898 | 2,747 | 6,582 | 3,497 | 8,677 |
    | x 8 | x 3 | x 5 | x 8 | x 7 |

Now . . .
1. Circle in green the largest product in row 1.
2. In row 2, use red to circle the product with a zero in the tens place.
3. Circle in blue the even numbered products in row 3.
4. In row 4, circle the product with three zeros using yellow.
5. Circle in orange the smallest product in row 5.
6. In row 6, use brown to circle the largest and smallest products.

Math

Name _____

Find each quotient. Then write the letter of the problem in the matching numbered blank to find the answer to the riddle below.

Ⓨ 1. $4\overline{)286}$ Ⓒ 2. $7\overline{)721}$ Ⓜ 3. $8\overline{)968}$ Ⓡ 4. $2\overline{)264}$ Ⓔ 5. $8\overline{)488}$

Ⓢ 6. $3\overline{)315}$ Ⓡ 7. $3\overline{)797}$ Ⓡ 8. $4\overline{)768}$ Ⓔ 9. $3\overline{)849}$ Ⓒ 10. $3\overline{)208}$

Ⓔ 11. $7\overline{)266}$ Ⓒ 12. $5\overline{)425}$ Ⓣ 13. $8\overline{)997}$ Ⓟ 14. $6\overline{)675}$ Ⓒ 15. $8\overline{)992}$

Ⓨ 16. $7\overline{)917}$ Ⓡ 17. $7\overline{)508}$ Ⓤ 18. $3\overline{)639}$ Ⓔ 19. $5\overline{)455}$ Ⓣ 20. $5\overline{)650}$

Ⓚ 21. $4\overline{)394}$ Ⓑ 22. $4\overline{)884}$ Ⓐ 23. $5\overline{)540}$ Ⓑ 24. $7\overline{)786}$ Ⓘ 25. $3\overline{)387}$

What new cookbook is on the bestsellers' list?

$\overline{12}\ \overline{8}\ \overline{18}\ \overline{3}\ \overline{22}\ \overline{16}$ $\overline{7}\ \overline{11}\ \overline{2}\ \overline{25}\ \overline{14}\ \overline{19}\ \overline{6}$

by $\overline{24}\ \overline{5}\ \overline{13}\ \overline{20}\ \overline{1}$ $\overline{10}\ \overline{4}\ \overline{23}\ \overline{15}\ \overline{21}\ \overline{9}\ \overline{17}$

Math

Name _____

The math teacher, Mrs. Numbers, needs your help in averaging math grades. Compute the average of each student.

Student	Grades					Average
1. Angie Addition	72	86	70	88	94	_____
2. Cal Calculator	100	98	96	97	94	_____
3. Dewey Decimal	84	72	83	76	80	_____
4. Freddy Fraction	71	77	83	70	74	_____
5. Mary Multiple	92	88	90	91	84	_____
6. Perry Perimeter	70	80	73	75	77	_____
7. Quincy Quotient	85	94	88	86	82	_____
8. Randy Radius	65	70	68	71	66	_____
9. Sarah Sphere	94	98	100	97	96	_____
10. Teri Triangle	89	75	92	83	91	_____

Math

Name _____

Draw the next four shapes in each pattern.

1.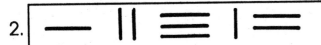

2.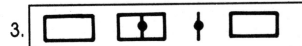

3.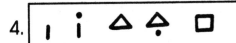

4.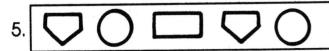

5.

6.

7.

8.

9.

10.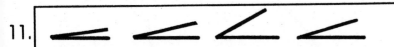

11.

12.

Math

Name _____

Write the correct term under each box.

Word Bank				
pyramid	sphere	intersecting lines	line	pentagon
hexagon	cone	parallelogram	octagon	right angle
rectangle	cube	rectangular prism	triangle	parallel lines
				cylinder

 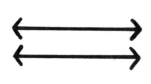  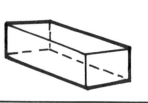

_____ _____ _____ _____

  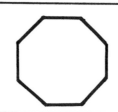 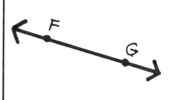

_____ _____ _____ _____

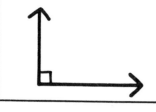  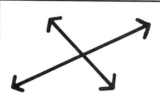 

_____ _____ _____ _____

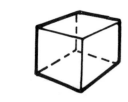   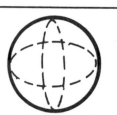

_____ _____ _____ _____

Math

Name _____

Write the perimeter inside each shape.

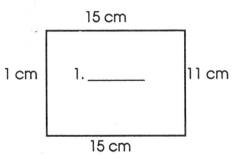

15 cm
1 cm   1._____   11 cm
15 cm

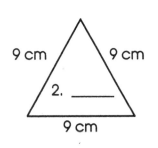

9 cm   9 cm
2. _____
9 cm

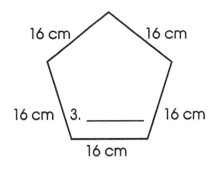

16 cm   16 cm
16 cm 3. _____ 16 cm
16 cm

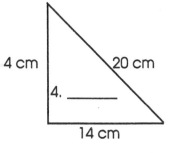

4 cm   20 cm
4._____
14 cm

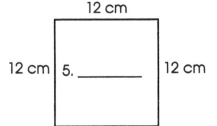

12 cm
12 cm 5._____ 12 cm
12 cm

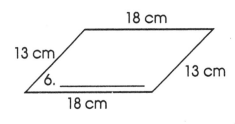

18 cm
13 cm   13 cm
6. _____
18 cm

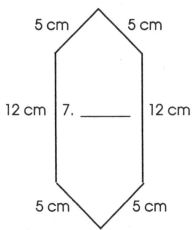

5 cm   5 cm
12 cm 7. _____ 12 cm
5 cm   5 cm

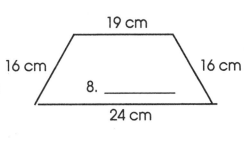

19 cm
16 cm   16 cm
8. _____
24 cm

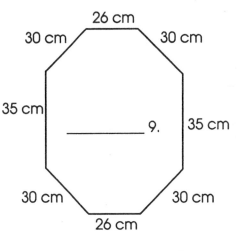

26 cm
30 cm   30 cm
35 cm   35 cm
_____ 9.
30 cm   30 cm
26 cm

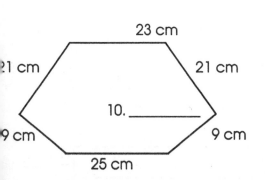

23 cm
21 cm   21 cm
10._____
9 cm   9 cm
25 cm

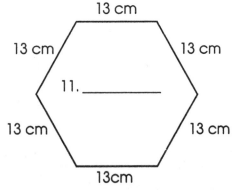

13 cm
13 cm   13 cm
11._____
13 cm   13 cm
13cm

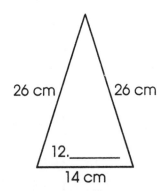

26 cm   26 cm
12._____
14 cm

Math

Name _____

Multiply to find the area of each carpet. **Area** = length x width

24 ft.

4 ft.

A = _____ sq. ft.

13 ft.

9 ft.

4 ft.

A = _____ sq. ft.

4 ft.

9 ft.

A = _____ sq. ft.

6 ft.

4 ft.

A = _____ sq. ft

9 ft.

9 ft.

A = _____ sq. ft.

6 ft.

17 ft.

A = _____ sq. ft.

30 ft.

3 ft.

A = _____ sq. ft.

7 ft.

16 ft.

A = _____ sq. ft.

15 ft.

8 ft.

A = _____ sq. ft.

26 ft.

2 ft.

A = _____ sq. ft.

Math

Name _____

Find each product.

47 x29	56 x13	79 x28	36 x73	48 x56	17 x44
62 x27	85 x43	33 x77	80 x12	59 x34	29 x54
57 x68	96 x27	88 x54	27 x54	88 x67	93 x26
842 x 16	665 x 28	748 x 34	893 x 56	667 x 45	854 x 18
394 x 76	746 x 17	377 x 28	858 x 33	972 x 75	631 x 14
291 x 26	179 x 66	814 x 27	485 x 89	349 x 58	723 x 44

Math

Name _____

Complete each equivalent fraction.

1. $\dfrac{2}{4} = \dfrac{}{8}$ 2. $\dfrac{3}{8} = \dfrac{}{16}$ 3. $\dfrac{1}{3} = \dfrac{}{6}$ 4. $\dfrac{3}{4} = \dfrac{}{16}$

5. $\dfrac{1}{2} = \dfrac{}{12}$ 6. $\dfrac{2}{7} = \dfrac{}{14}$ 7. $\dfrac{3}{9} = \dfrac{}{3}$ 8. $\dfrac{2}{5} = \dfrac{}{15}$

9. $\dfrac{1}{6} = \dfrac{}{12}$ 10. $\dfrac{3}{5} = \dfrac{}{15}$ 11. $\dfrac{1}{6} = \dfrac{}{2}$ 12. $\dfrac{3}{4} = \dfrac{}{12}$

13. $\dfrac{4}{5} = \dfrac{}{10}$ 14. $\dfrac{2}{6} = \dfrac{}{3}$ 15. $\dfrac{2}{3} = \dfrac{}{9}$ 16. $\dfrac{3}{5} = \dfrac{}{10}$

Compare these fractions (< > =).

1. $\dfrac{4}{5} \bigcirc \dfrac{2}{5}$ 2. $\dfrac{6}{10} \bigcirc \dfrac{1}{10}$ 3. $\dfrac{2}{6} \bigcirc \dfrac{1}{3}$

4. $\dfrac{1}{2} \bigcirc \dfrac{2}{4}$ 5. $\dfrac{2}{8} \bigcirc \dfrac{3}{4}$ 6. $\dfrac{1}{6} \bigcirc \dfrac{4}{6}$

7. $\dfrac{2}{8} \bigcirc \dfrac{1}{4}$ 8. $\dfrac{5}{8} \bigcirc \dfrac{2}{8}$ 9. $\dfrac{2}{10} \bigcirc \dfrac{4}{5}$

Write in the simplest terms.

1. $\dfrac{3}{6} = $ —   2. $\dfrac{4}{12} = $ —   3. $\dfrac{6}{9} = $ —   4. $\dfrac{4}{20} = $ —

5. $\dfrac{6}{10} = $ —   6. $\dfrac{5}{15} = $ —   7. $\dfrac{2}{8} = $ —   8. $\dfrac{2}{10} = $ —

9. $\dfrac{9}{12} = $ —   10. $\dfrac{8}{20} = $ —   11. $\dfrac{7}{14} = $ —   12. $\dfrac{9}{18} = $ —

Math

Name _____

Follow the directions to complete the line graph.

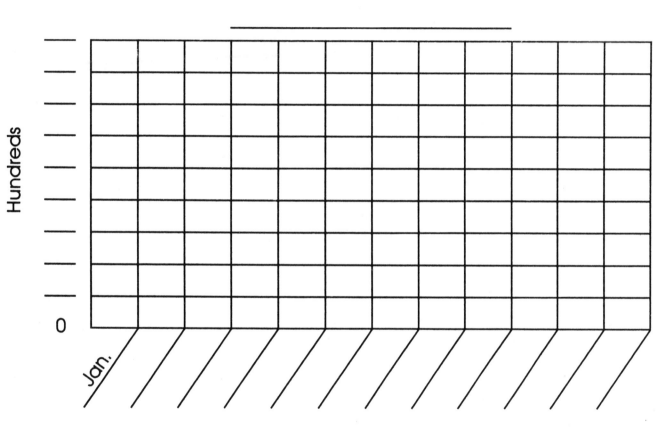

Hundreds

0

Jan.

1. Up the left side of the graph, number the Hundreds from 0 - 18, counting by twos.
2. On the diagonal lines, write each month beginning with January.
   Abbreviations may be used.
3. Above the graph, write the title **Banana Split Bonanza**.
4. Plot each point on the graph to show the number of banana splits sold
   each month.

Jan. – 4	May – 15	Sept. – 16
Feb. – 6	June – 17	Oct. – 13
March – 7	July – 18	Nov. – 12
April – 10	Aug. – 18	Dec. – 11

Math

Name _____

The bar graph shows how much candy was sold in a candy drive. Use the graph to answer the questions.

(There are 12 bars in each box.)

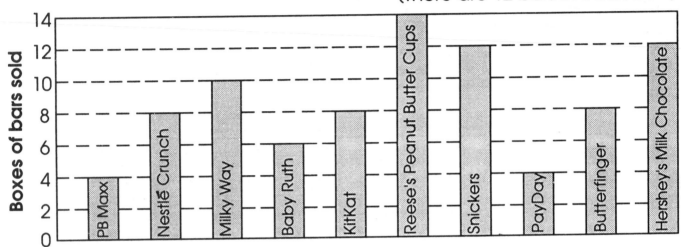

1. How many boxes of Snickers and Milky Ways were sold? _____

2. How many Hershey's bars were sold? _____

3. How many more KitKat bars than PB Maxx bars were sold? _____

4. Twelve boxes were sold of which candy bars? _____

   _____

5. How many Nestlé Crunch and Baby Ruth bars were sold? _____

6. How many more boxes of PayDays would have to be sold to equal the number of Hershey's boxes sold? _____

7. How many packages of Reese's cups were sold? _____

8. Less than 10 boxes were sold of which candy bars? _____

   _____

9. What is the difference in the amount of Milky Way and Butterfinger bars sold? _____

10. What is the total number of boxes sold in the candy drive? _____

*Challenge: What was the total number of candy bars sold? _____

Name _____

Fill in each box with +, –, x, or ÷ to make each math equation true.

1. 28 ☐ 4 ☐ 3 = 21

2. 7 ☐ 7 ☐ 5 = 44

3. 6 ☐ 3 ☐ 4 = 8

4. 72 ☐ 9 ☐ 4 = 32

5. 3 ☐ 3 ☐ 6 = 36

6. 56 ☐ 7 ☐ 4 = 32

7. 49 ☐ 7 ☐ 6 = 42

8. 42 ☐ 6 ☐ 8 = 15

9. 6 ☐ 6 ☐ 6 = 6

10. 8 ☐ 8 ☐ 28 = 36

11. 2 ☐ 7 ☐ 14 = 28

12. 16 ☐ 4 ☐ 12 = 24

13. 35 ☐ 7 ☐ 5 = 25

14. 11 ☐ 4 ☐ 1 = 6

15. 4 ☐ 4 ☐ 5 = 21

16. 6 ☐ 4 ☐ 7 = 14

17. 56 ☐ 7 ☐ 3 = 24

18. 9 ☐ 6 ☐ 4 = 58

19. 5 ☐ 4 ☐ 3 = 17

20. 2 ☐ 3 ☐ 4 = 10

21. 24 ☐ 6 ☐ 9 = 36

22. 12 ☐ 3 ☐ 9 = 81

23. 24 ☐ 8 ☐ 12 = 36

24. 72 ☐ 9 ☐ 8 = 1

Math

Name _____

Try these math puzzles for fun! Trace each shape on another piece of paper.
Follow the directions to form new shapes.

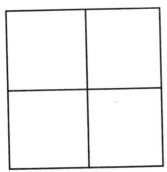

1. Erase 4 line segments
   to leave 1 square.

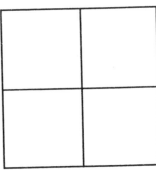

2. Erase 4 line segments
   to leave 2 squares.

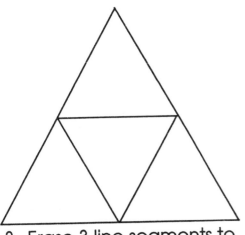

3. Erase 3 line segments to
   to leave 2 triangles.

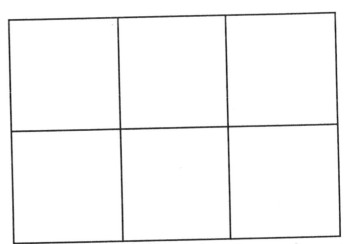

4. Erase 5 line segments to leave 3 squares.

Social Studies

Name _____

Unscramble and write each geographic term. Then draw a picture to illustrate the meaning of each term.

_____ (yalevl)	_____ (tiomuann)	_____ (oncayn)	_____ (noalvoc)
_____ (ohbrar)	_____ (lipan)	_____ (aceon)	_____ (tacos)
_____ (erirv)	_____ (uneplnais)	_____ (flug)	_____ (inctetonn)
_____ (ase)	_____ (tupaela)	_____ (daslin)	_____ (kale)

On a sheet of paper, write a short definition of each term.

Social Studies

Name _____

Find the year that each of these U.S. Presidents took office.
Then plot them on the time line in chronological order.

Presidents

G. Washington _____	A. Jackson _____	B. Clinton _____
T. Jefferson _____	H. Truman _____	R. Nixon _____
J. F. Kennedy _____	J. Carter _____	D. Eisenhower _____
F. D. Roosevelt _____	J. Madison _____	R. Reagan _____
Abe Lincoln _____	U. S. Grant _____	J. Q. Adams _____

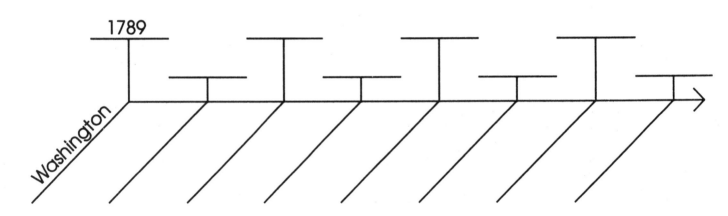

1789

Washington

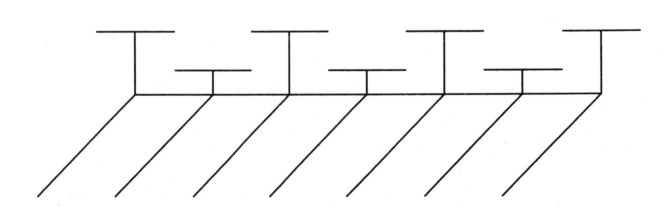

Social Studies

Name _____

ollow the directions to complete each globe.

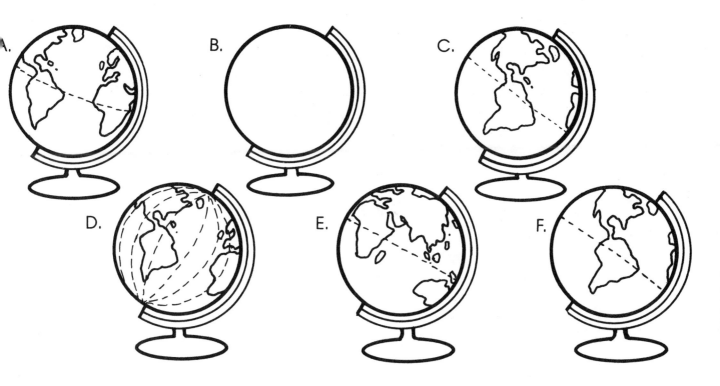

. Draw a red equator on Globe D to separate the northern and southern hemispheres.

. On Globe C, add red lines of longitude and blue lines of latitude.

. Color the continents of the western hemisphere on Globe F orange.

. Divide Globe A into the western and eastern hemispheres. Draw purple stripes in the western hemisphere and yellow polka dots in the eastern hemisphere.

. On Globe E, color the continents of the eastern hemisphere green.

. On Globe B, use five colors to write the name of our planet.

. List the seven continents. _____   _____

_____   _____   _____

_____   _____

. List the four major oceans. _____

_____   _____   _____

Social Studies

Name _____

Follow the directions to complete the map.

1. Label the seven continents.
2. Label the four major oceans.
3. There are three countries in North America. Color each one a different color. Their names are _____ , _____ , and _____ .
4. Color the largest country in South America yellow. It's name is _____ .
5. Color the large island NE of North America green. Its name is _____ .
6. Draw green stalks of rice in southeast Asia.
7. Outline China and draw diagonal brown stripes on it.
8. Name two European countries.   _____   _____
9. Draw a brown kangaroo on Australia.
10. Color the islands of Japan in pink.
11. Outline Africa in orange. Name its two countries that begin with the letter **E**.

    _____   _____
12. Draw a polar bear on the continent of Antarctica.

Social Studies

Name _____

ollow the directions to complete the map of the contiguous United States.

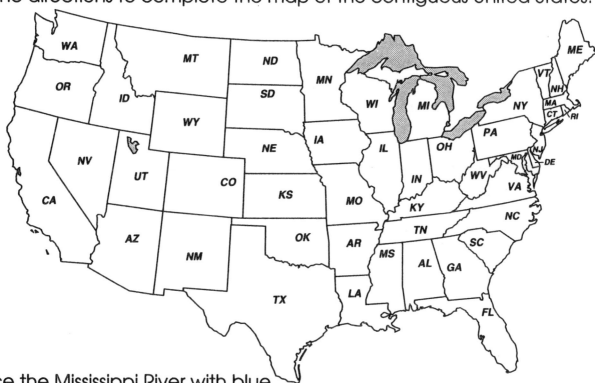

1. Trace the Mississippi River with blue.
2. Color the largest state with green polka dots. Its name is _____ .
3. Color the smallest state yellow. Its name is _____ .
4. Outline all states beginning with **A** orange.
5. Add these brown symbols (∧∧∧) for the Rocky Mountains.
6. Label the five Great Lakes by writing the first letter of each name in blue. Name them. _____ _____ _____ _____ _____
7. Put a green **2** on all states with two words in their names.
8. Put a red ★ on Washington, D.C., our nation's capital.
9. Outline the state where you live in black.
10. Put a red **V** on all states whose name starts with a vowel.
11. What country touches the U.S. on the north?_____ south?_____
12. What ocean touches the east coast? _____ west? _____
13. Put an orange **F** on the state that comes first in alphabetical order, and an orange **L** on the one that comes last. Name them. _____ _____
14. Draw a blue whale in the Gulf of Mexico.

Social Studies

Name _____

Label the map of the U.S. using the two letter postal abbreviations for each state.

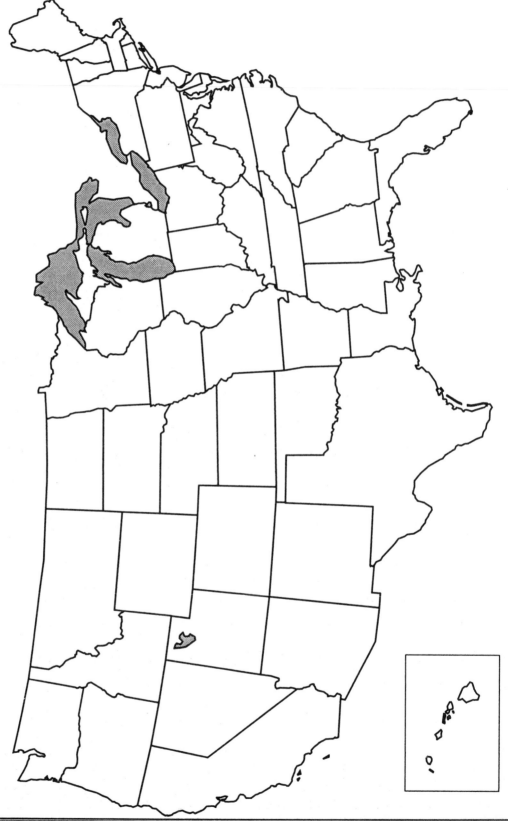

Social Studies

Name _____

Complete the information about your state.

1. Draw your state and write its name.

2. On your state label . . .
   - ✪ state capital
   - • 4 major cities
     (blue) rivers
     (blue) lakes
     (brown) mountains

State name _____

3. Your state nickname _____

4. Date of admission to the union _____

5. State motto _____

6. State bird _____

7. State flower_____

8. State tree _____

9. State song _____

10. Chief manufactured products _____

11. Natural resources _____

12. Interesting places to visit _____

   _____

   _____

13. States that border my state _____

14. Governor of my state _____

15. Draw your . . .

| state bird | state flower | state flag |

Social Studies

Name _____

Match each state with its capital.

STATES

Alabama	_15_	Indiana	___	Nebraska	___	South Carolina	___
Alaska	___	Iowa	___	Nevada	___	South Dakota	___
Arizona	___	Kansas	___	New Hampshire	___	Tennessee	___
Arkansas	___	Kentucky	___	New Jersey	___	Texas	___
California	___	Louisiana	___	New Mexico	___	Utah	___
Colorado	___	Maine	___	New York	___	Vermont	___
Connecticut	___	Maryland	___	North Carolina	___	Virginia	___
Delaware	___	Massachusetts	___	North Dakota	___	Washington	___
Florida	___	Michigan	___	Ohio	___	West Virginia	___
Georgia	___	Minnesota	___	Oklahoma	___	Wisconsin	___
Hawaii	___	Mississippi	___	Oregon	___	Wyoming	___
Idaho	___	Missouri	___	Pennsylvania	___		
Illinois	___	Montana	___	Rhode Island	___		

CAPITALS

1. Nashville	14. Boston	27. Bismarck	40. Santa Fe
2. Lansing	15. Montgomery	28. Little Rock	41. Trenton
3. Albany	16. Boise	29. Topeka	42. Oklahoma City
4. Juneau	17. Providence	30. Sacramento	43. Pierre
5. Springfield	18. Jefferson City	31. Denver	44. Madison
6. Atlanta	19. Olympia	32. Frankfort	45. Tallahassee
7. Harrisburg	20. Montpelier	33. Columbia	46. Indianapolis
8. Columbus	21. Phoenix	34. Concord	47. Hartford
9. Honolulu	22. Baton Rouge	35. Lincoln	48. Annapolis
10. Richmond	23. Des Moines	36. Charleston	49. Dover
11. Austin	24. Salem	37. Cheyenne	50. Augusta
12. Jackson	25. Carson City	38. Helena	
13. Raleigh	26. St. Paul	39. Salt Lake City	

Which capitals do you think could have been named to honor presidents of

the U.S.? _____

_____

Social Studies

Name _____

Use the lines of latitude and longitude to identify and to plot countries.

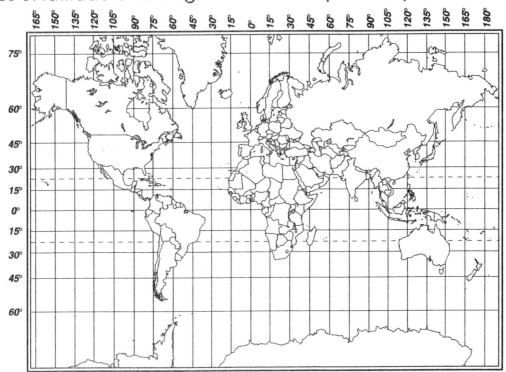

Give the country that is located approximately at each coordinate. Label the countries on the map.

1. 50°N - 0°   _____France_____
2. 40°N - 15°E _____
3. 40°N - 105°E _____
4. 35°N - 95°W _____
5. 0° - 20°E   _____

6. 20°S - 50°W   _____
7. 65°N - 20°W   _____
8. 55°N - 105°W _____
9. 30°S - 33°E   _____
10. 20°S - 140°E _____

Write the approximate latitude and longitude of each country.

1. Ecuador   ___0° - 80°W___
2. Madagascar _____
3. Indonesia   _____
4. Greenland   _____
5. India   _____

6. New Zealand _____
7. Japan   _____
8. Algeria   _____
9. Russia   _____
10. Ethiopia   _____

Social Studies

Name _____

Use the grid to answer the questions about Washington, D.C.

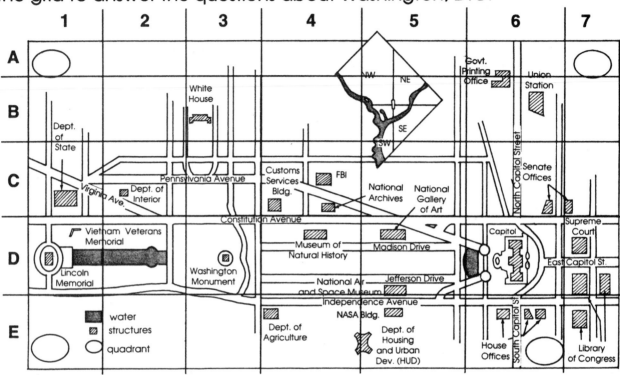

1. What famous residence is in B3? _____

2. The National Gallery of Art is in which grid? _____

3. Where is the U.S. Supreme Court? _____

4. What two things could you see at D1? _____ _____

5. What street runs between the House Offices in E6? _____

6. The FBI is located in section _____ .

7. Laws are made in the Capitol at _____ .

8. What museum could you visit in D4? _____

9. Where is the Washington Monument located? _____

10. What could you find in section B6? _____

11. What street runs horizontally through C3? _____

12. What government building is in section E4? _____

13. Jefferson Drive runs between which two sections? _____ _____

14. What street runs diagonally through sections C1 and C2? _____

Social Studies

Name _____

Use the Star-Spangled code to identify each famous American. Then match each person with his/her contribution to our country.

A B C D E F G H
4 17 13 8 1 20 15 10

I J K L M N O P
3 21 25 7 16 12 2 19

Q R S T U V W X Y Z
23 6 11 9 5 22 14 26 18 24

1. 17 - 1 - 12   20 - 6 - 4 - 12 - 25 - 7 - 3 - 12   _____

2. 13 - 7 - 4 - 6 - 4   17 - 4 - 6 - 9 - 2 - 12   _____

3. 10 - 1 - 12 - 6 - 18   20 - 2 - 6 - 8   _____

4. 6 - 2 - 11 - 4   19 - 4 - 6 - 25 - 11   _____

5. 10 - 4 - 6 - 6 - 3 - 1 - 9   9 - 5 - 17 - 16 - 4 - 12   _____

6. 4 - 16 - 1 - 7 - 3 - 4   1 - 4 - 6 - 10 - 4 - 6 - 9   _____

7. 9 - 10 - 2 - 16 - 4 - 11   1 - 8 - 3 - 11 - 2 - 12   _____

8. 11 - 4 - 7 - 7 - 18   6 - 3 - 8 - 1   _____

9. 20 - 6 - 4 - 12 - 13 - 3 - 11   11 - 13 - 2 - 9 - 9   25 - 1 - 18

_____

Contributions

___ helped free slaves through use of the Underground Railroad

___ founded the American Red Cross

___ proved with a kite that lightning is electricity

___ fought for equality of blacks

___ invented the electric light bulb

___ first American woman in space

___ wrote the words to our national anthem

___ developed the Model T car

___ first woman to cross the Atlantic Ocean by air

Science

Name _____

Unscramble each set of letters to learn more about rocks and minerals.

Minerals

There are about 3,000 minerals on earth. Minerals can be identified by the following properties:

a. _____
   (roolc)

c. _____
   (serult)

b. _____
   (kartes)

d. _____
   (sadenshr)

Rocks

Most rocks are mixtures of one or more minerals. Rocks are classified into three groups.

a. formed from cooled volcanic magma
   _____
   (ungisoe)

b. consist of layers of old rock, or plants and animal
   _____
   (tamyesdienr)

c. formed when minerals are changed by heat and pressure _____
   (pamichrotem)

Science

Name _____

Write the name of each animal baby beside the correct animal. Write the
letters from the boxes in the numbered blanks below to answer the riddle.

Word Bank				
chick	joey	cub	colt	gosling
eaglet	poult	fawn	cygnet	calf
foal	cub	kid	calf	

1. donkey __ ☐ __ __

2. kangaroo __ __ ☐ __

3. eagle __ __ __ __ __ ☐

4. turkey __ __ ☐ __ __

5. goose __ __ __ ☐ __ __ __

6. bear ☐ __ __

7. cattle __ ☐ __ __

8. fox __ ☐ __

9. swan ☐ __ __ __ __ __

10. goat __ __ ☐

11. deer __ __ __ ☐

12. elephant __ ☐ __ __

13. ostrich __ __ __ __ ☐

What duck has wings, feathers, and fangs?

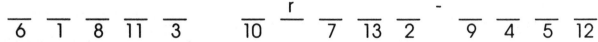

___ ___ ___ ___ ___   ___ r ___ ___ ___   - ___ ___ ___ ___
 6   1   8   11   3   10   7   13   2   9   4   5   12

Science

Name _____

Use the code to identify each group of animals. Write the word in the blank.

A	B	C	D	E	F	G	H	I	J	K	L	M
2	15	10	7	3	17	11	21	1	23	18	8	13

N	O	P	Q	R	S	T	U	V	W	X	Y	Z
24	4	14	22	12	6	9	5	16	25	19	20	26

1. a (17 - 8 - 4 - 10 - 18) of chickens _____

2. a (18 - 3 - 24 - 24 - 3 - 8) of dogs _____

3. a (6 - 10 - 21 - 4 - 4 - 8) of fish _____

4. a (6 - 18 - 5 - 8 - 18) of foxes _____

5. a (11 - 2 - 11 - 11 - 8 - 3) of geese _____

6. a (10 - 4 - 8 - 4 - 24 - 20) of ants _____

7. a (21 - 3 - 12 - 7) of whales _____

8. a (14 - 2 - 10 - 3) of donkeys _____

9. a (14 - 12 - 1 - 7 - 3) of lions _____

10. a (25 - 2 - 12 - 12 - 3 - 24) of rabbits _____

11. a (7 - 12 - 4 - 16 - 3) of cattle _____

12. a (10 - 8 - 4 - 25 - 7 - 3 - 12) of cats _____

13. a (7 - 12 - 4 - 16 - 3) of pigs _____

14. a (6 - 8 - 4 - 9 - 21) of bears _____

15. a (9 - 12 - 4 - 4 - 14) of kangaroos _____

16. a (14 - 2 - 10 - 18) of wolves _____

Science

Name _____

Write each answer on the matching plant leaf.

1. Food-making process of plants
2. Green substance in plants that uses sunlight to make food
3. Part of seed that stores food
4. Yellow powder of plants
5. Plants that grow year after year
6. A tiny cell that can grow into a plant
7. Plants that produce seeds in cones
8. Underground part that absorbs water and minerals
9. Plants that live for only one year
10. A gas plants need in order to live and grow
11. The main stalk of a plant
12. One who studies plants
13. Plants that live for two seasons

Word Bank

			root
carbon dioxide	pollen	perennials	botanist
photosynthesis	annuals	chlorophyll	conifers
cotyledon	spore	stem	biennials

Science

Name _____

Use the picture, the clue, and the scrambled letters to write the name of each dinosaur.

Thunder lizard

_____

(rutapusaosa)

Three-horned

_____

(treposartci)

Large flier

_____

(narotdepno)

Large thumb spike

_____

(daugnoion)

Single row of plates

_____

(gaesrtusuos)

Huge plant-eater

_____

(sarcbaruhoius)

Largest meat-eater

_____

(snotraysnurau)

Ostrich-like

_____

(hotmsronimui)

Covered with
armored plates

_____

(klsursanyoau)

Science

Name _____

Label each diagram. Color as directed.

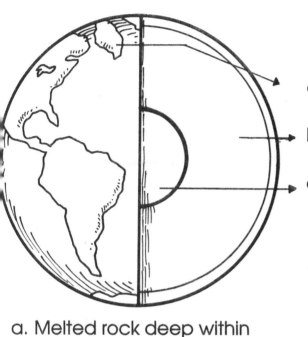

The Earth

a. _____ Outer layer of rock and soil (blue-green)

b. _____ Layer of rock under heat and pressure (orange)

c. _____ Melted iron and nickel around solid core (red)

A Volcano

a. _____

b. _____

c. _____

d. _____

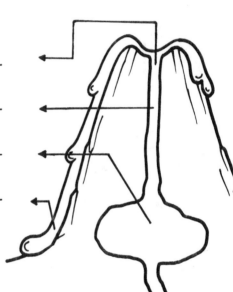

a. Melted rock deep within the earth (red)

b. Crack through which magma escapes (orange)

c. Where magma collects (yellow)

d. Melted rock that erupts from a volcano (black)

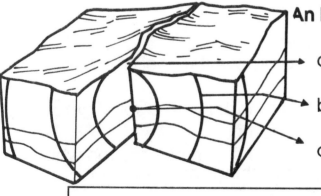

An Earthquake

a. _____ Point where stress is released (orange)

b. _____ Vibrations from the release of this stress (black)

c. _____ Place where shock waves first reach (red)

	Word Bank	
		focus
shock waves	mantle	crust
magma chamber	vent	lava
epicenter	core	magma

Science

Name _____

Complete the crossword puzzle.

Word Bank

simple machines	pulley	effort	lever
inclined plane	inertia	force	friction
wheel and axle	work	wedge	gravity
resistance	screw		

Across

3. devices with few moving parts that make work easier
6. causes moving objects to stay in motion
7. using force to move an object
9. applying force to move an object
10. the force used to do work
12. a bar used for prying
13. the pull toward earth's center
14. a handle and a stem

Down

1. a grooved wheel and a rope or chain
2. a cylinder with a spiral groove
4. a ramp
5. force that resists motion when two things rub together
8. triangular-shaped with an edge that tapers to a point
11. a push or a pull

IF8786 Fourth Grade in Review

Science

Name _____

Write each form of energy in the correct box.

Word Bank			
hair dryer	flute	mixer	toaster
sun	Ferris wheel	food	furnace
truck	train	laser	fire
batteries	oven	candle	thermometer
lamp	blender	wood	drum
fuel tank	jet	thunder	Niagara Falls

Heat Energy
_____
_____
_____
_____

Light Energy
_____
_____
_____
_____

Sound Energy
_____
_____
_____
_____

Electrical Energy
_____
_____
_____
_____

Stored Energy
_____
_____
_____
_____

Motion Energy
_____
_____
_____
_____

Science

Name _____

Write the answers in the blanks using the Word Banks.

Lunar Word Bank							
1/6	Apollo 11	seas	lunar rover	lunar	craters	reflected	phases

1. The moon's lowlands are called _____.

2. Many bowl-shaped _____ make up the moon's surface.

3. _____ refers to the moon.

4. ⬛🌒🌓🌗🌕🌔🌖🌘 Symbols represent the _____ of the moon

5. The moon has about _____ the gravity of the earth.

6. The moon's light is _____ from the sun.

7. _____ was the first U.S. spacecraft to land on the moon.

8. Astronauts traveled on the moon in a vehicle called a _____.

Solar Word Bank					
flare	million	sunspots	solar	365 days	heat
star	helium	hydrogen	light	white dwarf	

1. _____ means relating to the sun.

2. The sun gives earth _____ and _____.

3. The sun is really a _____.

4. The sun is made mostly of the gases _____ and _____

5. It takes earth _____ to orbit the sun.

6. Eventually, the sun will become a _____.

7. Dark regions on the sun are called _____.

8. A _____ may result from the eruption of the sun's gases.

9. The earth is about 93 _____ miles from the sun.

Science

Name _____

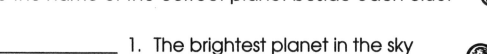

Write the name of the correct planet beside each clue.

_____ 1. The brightest planet in the sky

_____ 2. Closest to the sun

_____ 3. Has a large area known as the *Great Red Spot*

_____ 4. Is tipped over so far that it appears to roll

_____ 5. The smallest planet

_____ 6. The largest planet

_____ 7. Has living organisms

_____ 8. The second largest planet

_____ 9. Has at least 11 rings and is seventh from the sun

_____ 10. Water makes up 71% of the planet's surface

_____ 11. Eighth planet from the sun

_____ 12. Has huge volcanoes near its equator

_____ 13. 93 million miles from the sun

_____ 14. Once known as the *Evening Star*

_____ 15. Contains a dark area known as the *Great Dark Spot*

_____ 16. Spins so fast it bulges at its equator

_____ 17. Two-thirds of the planet is reddish-brown

Draw and label the planets in the correct order from the sun.

Science

Name _____

Someday you may be interested in a career in science. Use the code box to match the job descriptions with the career.

A	B	C	D	E	F	G	H	I	J	K	L	M
3	26	11	7	4	23	12	14	2	22	16	8	18

N	O	P	Q	R	S	T	U	V	W	X	Y	Z
9	1	15	20	5	19	6	10	25	13	24	17	21

1. I study animal life.

_____
(21 - 1 - 1 - 8 - 1 - 12 - 2 - 19 - 6)

2. I am a space pilot.

_____
(3 - 19 - 6 - 5 - 1 - 9 - 3 - 10 - 6)

3. Using our natural resources properly is my main concern.

_____
(11 - 1 - 9 - 19 - 4 - 5 - 25 - 3 - 6 - 2 - 1 - 9 - 2 - 19 - 6

4. I design circuitry.

_____
(4 - 8 - 4 - 11 - 6 - 5 - 2 - 11 - 3 - 8   4 - 9 - 12 - 2 - 9 - 4 - 4 - 5

5. I study plant life.

_____
(26 - 1 - 6 - 3 - 9 - 2 - 19 - 6)

6. The universe is my area of study.

_____
(3 - 19 - 6 - 5 - 1 - 9 - 1 - 18 - 4 - 5)

7. I study the origin of human beings.

_____
(3 - 9 - 6 - 14 - 5 - 1 - 15 - 1 - 8 - 1 - 12 - 2 - 19 - 6

8. The recovery and study of the remains of a past culture is my job.

_____
(3 - 5 - 11 - 14 - 3 - 4 - 1 - 8 - 1 - 12 - 2 - 19 - 6

9. I mix different kinds of matter to make new materials.

_____
(11 - 14 - 4 - 18 - 2 - 11 - 3 - 8   4 - 9 - 12 - 2 - 9 - 4 - 4 - 5)

10. I study and forecast weather.

_____
(18 - 4 - 6 - 4 - 1 - 5 - 1 - 8 - 1 - 12 - 2 - 19 - 6

11. Rocks and minerals are my interests.

_____
(12 - 4 - 1 - 8 - 1 - 12 - 2 - 19 - 6)

12. I design machines using heat and power.

_____
(18 - 4 - 11 - 14 - 3 - 9 - 2 - 11 - 3 - 8   4 - 9 - 12 - 2 - 9 - 4 - 4 - 5

Answer Key
Fourth Grade
in Review

Reading

Name _____

Follow the arrows to mark the vowels in each word long or short. Then color the arrows according to the code.

yellow ā

ă black

green ē

ĕ red

white ī

ĭ pink

gold ō

ŏ orange

blue ū

ŭ purple

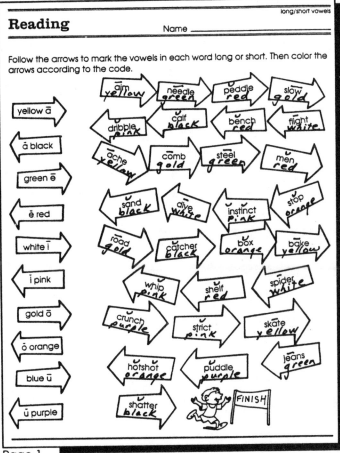

Page 1

Reading

Name _____

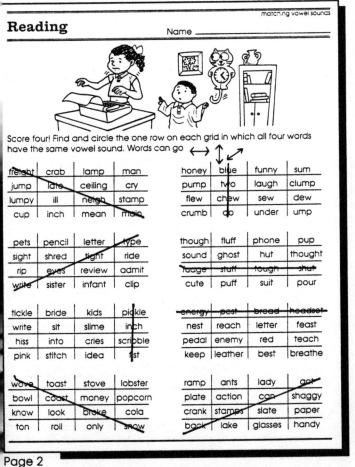

Score four! Find and circle the one row on each grid in which all four words have the same vowel sound. Words can go ←→ ↑↓ ↗

freight	crab	lamp	man
jump	late	ceiling	cry
lumpy	ill	neigh	stamp
cup	inch	mean	main

honey	blue	funny	sum
pump	two	laugh	clump
flew	chew	sew	dew
crumb	do	under	ump

pets	pencil	letter	type
sight	shred	tight	ride
rip	eyes	review	admit
write	sister	infant	clip

though	fluff	phone	pup
sound	ghost	hut	thought
fudge	stuff	tough	shut
cute	puff	suit	pour

tickle	bride	kids	pickle
write	sit	slime	inch
hiss	into	cries	scribble
pink	stitch	idea	fist

energy	pest	bread	headset
nest	reach	letter	feast
pedal	enemy	red	teach
keep	leather	best	breathe

wove	toast	stove	lobster
bowl	coast	money	popcorn
know	look	broke	cola
ton	roll	only	snow

ramp	ants	lady	got
plate	action	can	shaggy
crank	stamps	slate	paper
back	lake	glasses	handy

Page 2

Reading

Name _____

Use the clues to discover the double-letter alphabet words below. Write each word in the space provided.

AA = _aardvark_ African mammal
BB = _rabbit_ synonym for hare or bunny
CC = _raccoon_ masked animal with ringed tail
DD = _hidden_ not in sight
EE = _cheetah_ fastest land animal
FF = _stuffing_ bread cooked inside a turkey
GG = _egg_ where a yellow yolk is found
HH = _hitchhike_ to thumb a ride
II = _skiing_ sliding down a snowy slope
LL = _shell_ the home of a hermit crab
MM = _hammer_ a pounding tool
NN = _funny_ humorous
OO = _cookie_ a chocolate chip treat
PP = _hippo_ large water mammal
RR = _sorry_ feeling bad about something you did
SS = _crossword_ across and down clue-type puzzle
TT = _shuttle_ a spacecraft that lands like an airplane
UU = _vacuum_ a sweeper
ZZ = _drizzle_ light rain

Bonus: Find additional double-letter words for the letters listed.

Page 3

Reading

Name _____

Read the facts and opinions about Abe Lincoln and George Washington. If the statement is a fact, underline the sentence with blue. If it is an opinion, draw a red circle around the sentence.

1. Washington should not have owned slaves.
2. Abe Lincoln was the best president ever.
3. Lincoln was shot at Ford's Theatre.
4. Mount Vernon was the most beautiful presidential home.
5. Lincoln wrote the Gettysburg Address.
6. Abe felt that slavery was wrong.
7. Washington did not live in the White House.
8. Lincoln was taller than Washington.
9. I think George Washington was a great war general.
10. Abe was tall and skinny.
11. Lincoln was the 16th president of the United States.
12. George Washington was born on a plantation.
13. Some people thought Washington chopped down his father's cherry tree.
14. Abe Lincoln's nickname was "Honest Abe."

Page 4

Reading

Name _____

The main idea of a paragraph tells what the paragraph is about. Supporting details are sentences that explain the main idea. Write a paragraph for each main idea. Write the main idea first, then write three supporting sentences for each.

Main Ideas

1. Hawaii is a popular tourist site.
2. Computer games can challenge kids' minds.
3. Dolphins are intelligent animals.

1. _Paragraphs will vary._
_____
_____
_____
_____

2. _____
_____
_____
_____
_____

3. _____
_____
_____
_____

Page 5

Reading

Name _____

Number the baseball action sentences in proper sequence. Then illustrate the third sentence in each group in the matching home plate below.

A.
3 He threw a slider.
1 The pitcher walked to the mound.
2 He went into his wind-up.

C.
1 The batter selected his bat from the bat rack.
2 He rubbed pine tar on the handle.
3 He stepped into the batter's box.

B.
2 The ground crew covered the field with the tarp.
1 Dark clouds formed.
3 Heavy rain pelted the ground.

D.
2 It was time for the 7th inning stretch.
3 There were fireworks at the end of the game.
1 "The Star-Spangled Banner" started the game.

A.   C.

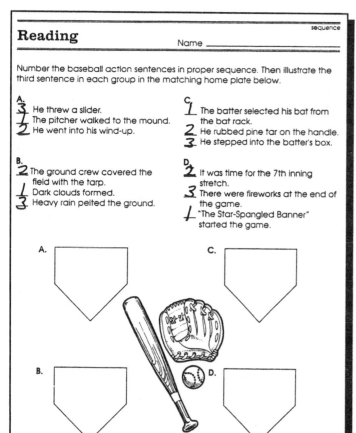

B.   D.

Page 6

Reading

Name _____

Write each word putting a dot between each syllable.

1. tarantula ta·ran·tu·la
2. spaniel span·iel
3. company com·pan·y
4. freckle freck·le
5. violin vi·o·lin
6. dandelion dan·de·li·on
7. labrador lab·ra·dor
8. sunflower sun·flow·er
9. alligator al·li·ga·tor
10. piccolo pic·co·lo
11. davenport dav·en·port

12. tomorrow to·mor·row
13. governor gov·er·nor
14. numeral nu·mer·al
15. beginning be·gin·ning
16. chrysanthemum chry·san·the·mum
17. quarrel quar·rel
18. woodpecker wood·peck·er
19. python py·thon
20. eskimo Es·ki·mo
21. potato po·ta·to
22. congratulations con·grat·u·la·tions

Page 7

Reading

Name _____

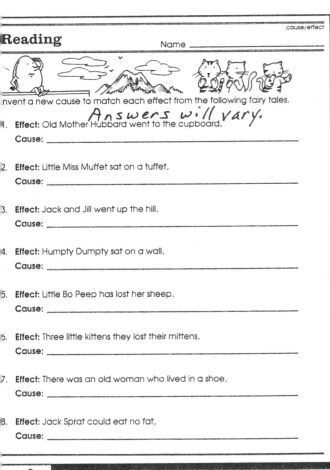

Invent a new cause to match each effect from the following fairy tales.

Answers will vary.

1. **Effect:** Old Mother Hubbard went to the cupboard,
   Cause: _____

2. **Effect:** Little Miss Muffet sat on a tuffet,
   Cause: _____

3. **Effect:** Jack and Jill went up the hill,
   Cause: _____

4. **Effect:** Humpty Dumpty sat on a wall,
   Cause: _____

5. **Effect:** Little Bo Peep has lost her sheep,
   Cause: _____

6. **Effect:** Three little kittens they lost their mittens,
   Cause: _____

7. **Effect:** There was an old woman who lived in a shoe,
   Cause: _____

8. **Effect:** Jack Sprat could eat no fat,
   Cause: _____

Reading

Name _____

Add the correct prefix. Then write the new word. In some cases more than one prefix can be used.

in	un	dis	re	im	mis

1. _in_ side — inside
2. _dis_ approve — disapprove
3. _dis_ like un. — dislike
4. _re_ take mis — retake
5. _un_ wind re — unwind
6. _im_ patient — impatient
7. _un_ safe — unsafe
8. _in_ visible — invisible
9. _dis_ connect — disconnect
10. _un_ beaten — unbeaten
11. _dis_ believe — disbelieve
12. _dis_ honest — dishonest
13. _mis_ print re — misprint
14. _im_ mature — immature
15. _re_ write — rewrite
16. _im_ proper — improper
17. _im_ possible — impossible
18. _in_ dependent — independent
19. _mis_ understood — misunderstood
20. _im_ practical — impractical
21. _un_ cover re — uncover
22. _dis_ regard — disregard

Reading

Name _____

Use the Word Bank to fill in the blanks with words containing suffixes. Put each boxed letter in the matching numbered blank below to find the state you might visit to get something necessary for school.

Word Bank

invitation	penniless	wonderful	hopeless
careful	noisy	collection	peaceful
addition	followed	winning	

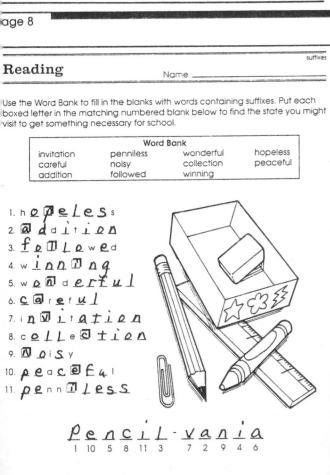

1. h o p e l e s s
2. a d d i t i o n
3. f o l l o w e d
4. w i n n i n g
5. w o n d e r f u l
6. c a r e f u l
7. i n v i t a t i o n
8. c o l l e c t i o n
9. n o i s y
10. p e a c e f u l
11. p e n n i l e s s

P e n c i l - v a n i a
1 10 5 8 11 3   7 2 9 4 6

Reading

Name _____

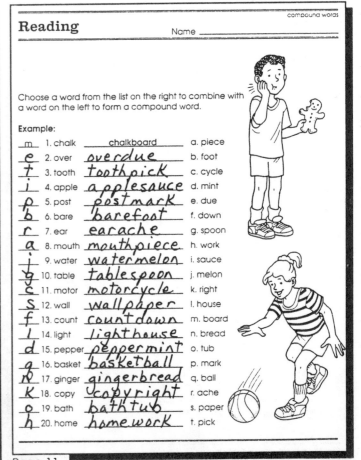

Choose a word from the list on the right to combine with a word on the left to form a compound word.

Example:

_m_ 1. chalk — chalkboard — a. piece
_e_ 2. over — overdue — b. foot
_t_ 3. tooth — toothpick — c. cycle
_i_ 4. apple — applesauce — d. mint
_p_ 5. post — postmark — e. due
_b_ 6. bare — barefoot — f. down
_r_ 7. ear — earache — g. spoon
_a_ 8. mouth — mouthpiece — h. work
_j_ 9. water — watermelon — i. sauce
_g_ 10. table — tablespoon — j. melon
_c_ 11. motor — motorcycle — k. right
_s_ 12. wall — wallpaper — l. house
_f_ 13. count — countdown — m. board
_l_ 14. light — lighthouse — n. bread
_d_ 15. pepper — peppermint — o. tub
_q_ 16. basket — basketball — p. mark
_n_ 17. ginger — gingerbread — q. ball
_k_ 18. copy — copyright — r. ache
_o_ 19. bath — bathtub — s. paper
_h_ 20. home — homework — t. pick

Page 12

Name _____

Find your way through the forest of contractions by writing the contraction in the tree and the letters the apostrophe replaces on the trunk.

Example:

can't	wouldn't	weren't	there's
o	o	o	i
can + not	would + not	were + not	there + is

it'll	let's	they'll	they've
wi	u	wi	ha
it + will	let + us	they + will	they + have

who's	they'd	she'll	doesn't
i	woul	wi	o
who + is	they + would	she + will	does + not

what's	haven't	here's	couldn't
i	o	i	o
what + is	have + not	here + is	could + not

Page 13

Name _____

Write each group of words in alphabetical order. Then write the correct words in the matching spaces at the bottom of the page to find out what Daisy Duck's father said to the shop clerk on the day of Daisy's wedding.

A. opossum
once
on
otter

1. on
2. once
3. opossum
4. otter

E. issue
it
inch
innocent

1. inch
2. innocent
3. issue
4. it

B. put
purse
pump
puddle

1. puddle
2. pump
3. purse
4. put

F. duty
dusty
dump
"ducks-edo"

1. "ducks-edo"
2. dump
3. dusty
4. duty

C. mask
myself
marble
my

1. marble
2. mask
3. my
4. myself

G. bird
binder
biggest
bill

1. biggest
2. bill
3. binder
4. bird

D. wrong
wrap
wrote
wrist

1. wrap
2. wrist
3. wrong
4. wrote

H. my
money
most
Mylar

1. money
2. most
3. my
4. Mylar

I. plead
plea
please
pleasure

1. plea
2. plead
3. please
4. pleasure

Answer: Please wrap my "ducks-edo" and put it on my bill.
I3   D1   H2   F1   B4   E4   A1   C3   G2

Page 14

Name _____

Follow the directions.

In triangle...

D – draw a green tricycle.
C – draw and color the "Three Blind Mice."
F – write a three-word tongue twister.
I – write three states whose names begin with M.
B – write today's date using only numbers.
E – draw a Triceratops.
L – write the Roman numerals for 3, 30, and 300.
H – write the names of the three summer months.
A – draw George Washington's tricorn hat.
K – write a class motto using three words.
J – draw a spotted cat using three colors.
G – design a pattern using three primary colors.

Page 15

Name _____

Write the letter of the alphabet that comes alphabetically after each letter given to identify these famous cartoon characters. Then cut out a speech bubble at the bottom. Match it with the cartoon character who would most likely make that comment.

Where are you, Calvin?	Watch me get Odie!	Mr. Wilson, where are you?
GNAADR	FZQEHDKC	CDMMHR the LDMZBD
Hobbes	Garfield	Dennis the Menace

Meet my buddy, Woodstock.	What's up, Doc?	Nothing ever goes right for me.
RMNNOX	ATFR ATMMX	YHFFX
Snoopy	Bugs Bunny	Ziggy

I'll change in this phone booth.	I tawt I taw a puddy tat!	I'm "all ears." Minnie.
RTODQL ZM	SVDDSX AHQC	LHBJDX LNTRD
Superman	Tweety Bird	Mickey Mouse

Reading

Name _____

Use the editing marks to correct the book review. Then write the story correctly on another paper.

Editing Marks		
◯ check spelling	ℓ cross out	∧ add	/ lower case letter
≡ capital letter	◯↗ move	¶ indent	

twenty-seven-year-old jackie robinson made baseball (historie) on april 15, 1947. he became the first black man to play (mager) (leage) baseball in the twentieth century jackie had to endure (numerus) insults from those those who felt only white men should play (mager) (leage) baseball but when he was hired by the dodgers jackie promised owner branch rickey that would have the guts not to (fite) back no jackie was a man who demanded respect he made (thot) promise and adhered (two) it so other black player (mite) follow in his footsteps today, black baseball players (everwhere) credit the (curage) and sacrifices of a (grate) man jackie robinson, the first to cross the (coler) line.

* Jackie Robinson and the Story of All-Black Baseball by Jim O'Connor

---

Reading

Name _____

Dial these famous pairs. **Example:** DIAL = 2 3 1 4

A B C 1	D E F 2	G H I 3
J K L 4	M N O 5	P Q R 6
S T U 7	V W X 8	Y Z 9

1. 1 1 7 5 1 5 and 6 5 1 3 5 — Batman & Robin
2. 3 1 5 7 2 4 and 3 6 2 7 2 4 — Hansel & Gretel
3. 4 1 1 4 and 4 3 4 4 — Jack & Jill
4. 6 1 5 5 5 1 and 1 2 2 9 7 7 — Ramona & Beezus
5. 4 7 1 9 and 2 2 7 3 — Lucy & Desi
6. 4 2 6 5 3 7 and 5 3 7 7 6 3 3 3 9 — Kermit & Miss Piggy
7. 1 2 1 7 7 9 and the 1 2 1 7 7 — Beauty & the Beast
8. 1 1 4 8 3 5 and 3 5 1 1 2 7 — Calvin & Hobbes
9. 5 3 5 5 3 2 and 5 3 1 4 2 9 5 5 7 7 2 — Minnie & Mickey Mouse
10. 4 1 2 9 and the 7 6 1 5 6 — Lady & the Tramp
11. 7 5 5 5 6 9 and 1 3 1 6 4 3 2 1 6 5 8 5 — Snoopy & Charlie Brown
12. 3 2 5 6 9 and 6 3 1 7 9 — Henry & Ribsy

Creative Writing

Name _____

Did you ever wonder what teachers do when they aren't with their students? Use imagination to write what they might do . . .

on vacation   Answers will vary.   in their car

at a teacher's meeting _____   at the grocery store _____

in their backyard _____   at a friend's home _____

at a football game _____   at a restaurant _____

Creative Writing

Name _____

$\frac{4}{5}$

Write a story about pies.

Your teacher is ill and the principal cannot locate a substitute. You have been asked to take her place for the day. Write your lesson plans.

Subject   Plans will vary.   Assignment

	Subject	Assignment
7:45 - 8:00		
8:00 - 8:30		
8:30 - 9:00		
9:00 - 9:30		
9:30 - 10:30		
10:30 - 11:00		
11:00 - 11:30		
11:30 - 12:30		
12:30 - 1:00		
1:00 - 1:30		
1:30 - 2:00		
2:00 - 2:30		
2:30 - 3:00		

Creative Writing

Name _____

Pretend that your pet could talk. Write what its answer would be to each question.

Answers will vary.

1. What type of animal are you? _____
2. What is your full name? _____
3. What do you like to be called? _____
4. What is your favorite expression? _____
5. What's your pet peeve? _____
6. What food do you most like to eat? _____
7. What is your favorite game? _____
8. Where do you most like to sleep? _____
9. What is your worst habit? _____
10. What is your favorite animal? _____
11. What is your favorite TV show? _____
12. What is your favorite toy? _____
13. What is your favorite place in the house? _____
14. Why don't you talk in front of anyone else? _____

Page 20

Creative Writing

Name _____

Your school has an exchange student from ancient Egypt – a mummy! Write about his adventures in your school. Include what can you learn from him.

Adventures will vary.

_____
_____
_____
_____
_____
_____
_____
_____
_____
_____
_____
_____

Design a tomb for the mummy to reside in when you take him back to Egypt.

Page 21

Creative Writing

Name _____

Did you ever want to give advice to your parents? Well, now is your chance. Write your tips on how to be a perfect parent.

1. *Tips will vary.*
2. _____
3. _____
4. _____
5. _____
6. _____
7. _____
8. _____
9. _____
10. _____

Page 22

Creative Writing

Name _____

Lights! Camera! Action! You are a movie critic. Write a review of your favorite movie. Then illustrate a scene from the beginning, middle, and end of the movie.

Movie Title _____

Reviews will vary.

_____
_____
_____
_____
_____
_____
_____
_____
_____
_____

Beginning	Middle	End

Page 23

Critical Thinking

Name _____

You have just won $100,000 in the Lucky Lotto. However, to keep the money, you must buy something for each of the following people and animals. Draw what you would give to each.

Illustrations will vary.

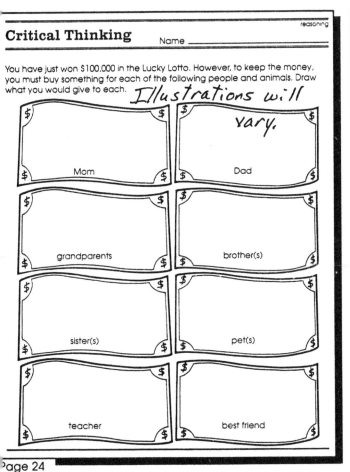

Mom	Dad
grandparents	brother(s)
sister(s)	pet(s)
teacher	best friend

Page 24

Critical Thinking

Name _____

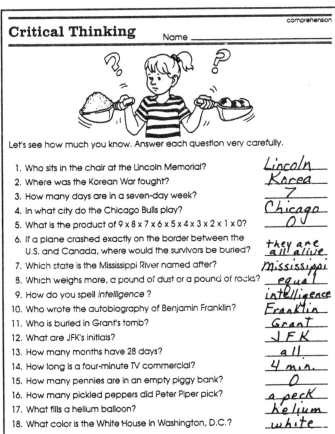

Let's see how much you know. Answer each question very carefully.

1. Who sits in the chair at the Lincoln Memorial? — *Lincoln*
2. Where was the Korean War fought? — *Korea*
3. How many days are in a seven-day week? — *7*
4. In what city do the Chicago Bulls play? — *Chicago*
5. What is the product of 9 x 8 x 7 x 6 x 5 x 4 x 3 x 2 x 1 x 0? — *0 ✓*
6. If a plane crashed exactly on the border between the U.S. and Canada, where would the survivors be buried? — *they are all alive*
7. Which state is the Mississippi River named after? — *Mississippi*
8. Which weighs more, a pound of dust or a pound of rocks? — *equal*
9. How do you spell *intelligence*? — *intelligence*
10. Who wrote the autobiography of Benjamin Franklin? — *Franklin*
11. Who is buried in Grant's tomb? — *Grant*
12. What are JFK's initials? — *JFK*
13. How many months have 28 days? — *all*
14. How long is a four-minute TV commercial? — *4 min.*
15. How many pennies are in an empty piggy bank? — *0*
16. How many pickled peppers did Peter Piper pick? — *a peck*
17. What fills a helium balloon? — *helium*
18. What color is the White House in Washington, D.C.? — *white*

Page 25

English

Name _____

These sentences make no sense because the words are not in the correct order. Write the sentences correctly beginning with the word that is capitalized and underlined.

1. changed the earth much during The million hundred last years has five
   The earth has changed much during the last five hundred million years.
2. lived 400 fish that ago About had gills both million there years lungs and
   About 400 million years ago there lived fish that had both gills and lungs.
3. forming ago Coral began years 410 reefs million
   Coral began forming reefs 410 million years ago.
4. quickly sail fin the heat Dimetrodon sun's large The collected on the
   The large sail fin on the Dimetrodon quickly collected the sun's heat.
5. ago 245 years Age The began million Reptiles about of
   The Age of Reptiles began about 245 million years ago.
6. reptile word means terrible dinosaur The
   The word dinosaur means terrible reptile.
7. Brachiosaurus tallest time was the animal of known all The
   The Brachiosaurus was the tallest known animal of all time.
8. 150 ago known the years oldest about bird million Archaeopteryx The appeared
   The oldest known bird, the Archaeopteryx, appeared about 150 million years ago.
9. vicious Tyrannosaurus a was The dinosaur meat-eating
   The Tyrannosaurus was a vicious meat-eating dinosaur.
10. Scientists extinct not are became dinosaurs sure the why
    Scientists are not sure why the dinosaurs became extinct.
11. appeared million plants ago Flowering 138 years
    Flowering plants appeared 138 million years ago.
12. prehistoric are stone in tell Fossils prints us about animals that and plants
    Fossils are prints in stone that tells us about prehistoric plants and animals.

Page 26

English

Name _____

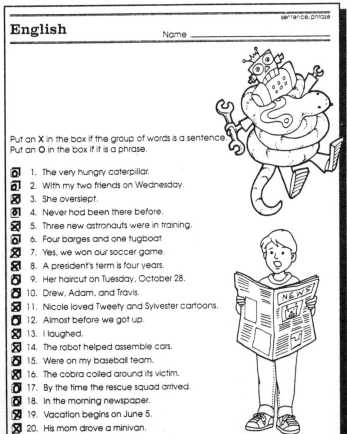

Put an X in the box if the group of words is a sentence.
Put an O in the box if it is a phrase.

1. O — The very hungry caterpillar.
2. O — With my two friends on Wednesday.
3. X — She overslept.
4. O — Never had been there before.
5. X — Three new astronauts were in training.
6. O — Four barges and one tugboat.
7. X — Yes, we won our soccer game.
8. X — A president's term is four years.
9. O — Her haircut on Tuesday, October 28.
10. O — Drew, Adam, and Travis.
11. X — Nicole loved Tweety and Sylvester cartoons.
12. O — Almost before we got up.
13. X — I laughed.
14. X — The robot helped assemble cars.
15. O — Were on my baseball team.
16. X — The cobra coiled around its victim.
17. O — By the time the rescue squad arrived.
18. O — In the morning newspaper.
19. X — Vacation begins on June 5.
20. X — His mom drove a minivan.

Page 27

English

Name _____

Draw a different colored line between the subject and predicate of each sentence.

1. You can visit Disney's Magic Kingdom in California or in Florida.
2. The San Diego Zoo is one of our country's best.
3. The Leaning Tower of Pisa in Italy has been leaning for over 600 years!
4. The Space Needle in Seattle, Washington, was built for the 1962 World's Fair.
5. The Statue of Liberty stands on Liberty Island in New York Harbor.
6. The Stone Mountain Memorial near Atlanta, Georgia, honors three famous Southern leaders.
7. Huge statues of Paul Bunyan and Babe the Blue Ox can be seen in Bemidji, Minnesota.
8. Plymouth Rock lies protected in Plymouth, Massachusetts.
9. Mount Vernon, Virginia, was the home of George Washington.
10. The Maid of the Mist is a boat that takes you very close to the bottom of Niagara Falls.
11. The statue of the Great Sphinx in Egypt has the head of a man and the body of a lion.
12. Water collected in the hole of a volcano to form Crater Lake in Oregon.

Page 28

English

Name _____

Read each sentence. Write **S** for statement, **C** for command, **Q** for question, and **E** for exclamation. Then add the end punctuation mark. Finally, draw the correct design in each box.

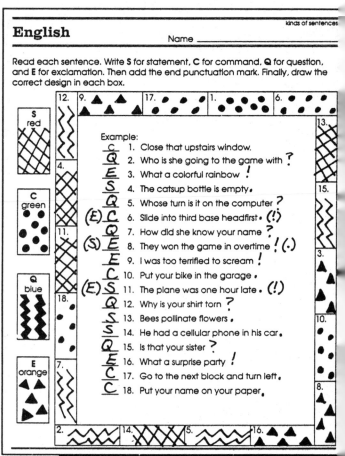

Example:
- C   1. Close that upstairs window.
- Q   2. Who is she going to the game with ?
- E   3. What a colorful rainbow !
- S   4. The catsup bottle is empty.
- Q   5. Whose turn is it on the computer ?
- (E) C   6. Slide into third base headfirst . (!)
- Q   7. How did she know your name ?
- (S) E   8. They won the game in overtime ! (.)
- E   9. I was too terrified to scream !
- C   10. Put your bike in the garage .
- (E) S   11. The plane was one hour late . (!)
- Q   12. Why is your shirt torn ?
- S   13. Bees pollinate flowers .
- S   14. He had a cellular phone in his car .
- Q   15. Is that your sister ?
- E   16. What a surprise party !
- C   17. Go to the next block and turn left .
- C   18. Put your name on your paper .

Page 29

English

Name _____

Choose a synonym from the Word Bank for each word on a Popsicle. Write it on the other half. Then color the half of the popsicle whose word comes first in alphabetical order.

Word Bank			
refuse	occur	shake	choose
purchase	fright	rough	reply
copy	vacant	worth	pledge
genuine	depart	simple	tardy

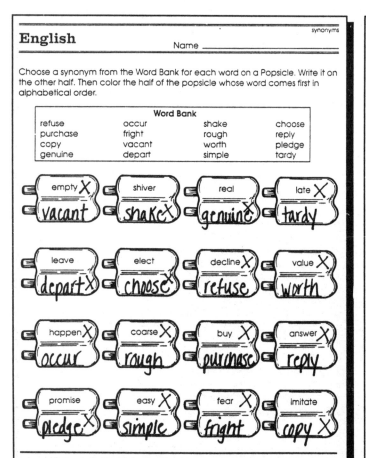

Page 30

English

Name _____

Write the matching antonym for each word.

Word Bank					
innocent	present	interior	victory	doubt	rare
defense	increase	shallow	few	wild	plain
departure	minimum	excited	lazy	smooth	rude

common **rare**   fancy **plain**   absent **present**

deep **shallow**   many **few**   maximum **minimum**

rough **smooth**   polite **rude**   arrival **departure**

ambitious **lazy**   decrease **increase**   offense **defense**

exterior **interior**   defeat **victory**   believe **doubt**

calm **excited**   guilty **innocent**   tame **wild**

Page 31

Write the correct homonym in the matching room of the Homonym Hotel.

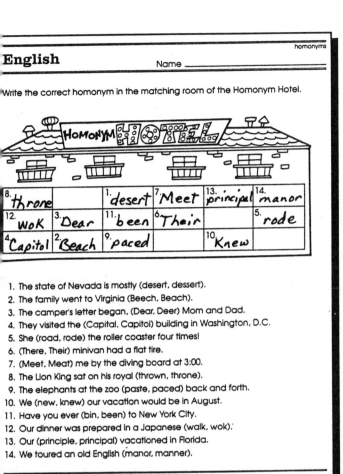

HOMONYM **HOTEL**

8. throne	1. desert	7. Meet	13. principal	14. manor
12. wok	3. Dear	11. been	6. Their	5. rode
4. Capitol	2. Beach	9. paced		10. Knew

1. The state of Nevada is mostly (desert, dessert).
2. The family went to Virginia (Beech, Beach).
3. The camper's letter began, (Dear, Deer) Mom and Dad.
4. They visited the (Capital, Capitol) building in Washington, D.C.
5. She (road, rode) the roller coaster four times!
6. (There, Their) minivan had a flat tire.
7. (Meet, Meat) me by the diving board at 3:00.
8. The Lion King sat on his royal (thrown, throne).
9. The elephants at the zoo (paste, paced) back and forth.
10. We (new, knew) our vacation would be in August.
11. Have you ever (bin, been) to New York City.
12. Our dinner was prepared in a Japanese (walk, wok).
13. Our (principle, principal) vacationed in Florida.
14. We toured an old English (manor, manner).

Use a dictionary to chart the information.

Answers will vary.

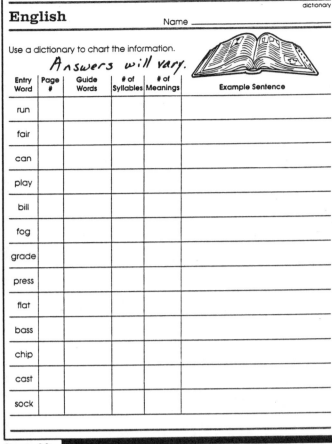

Entry Word	Page #	Guide Words	# of Syllables	# of Meanings	Example Sentence
run					
fair					
can					
play					
bill					
fog					
grade					
press					
flat					
bass					
chip					
cast					
sock					

Circle the words that would appear between each pair of guide words.

lemon - lilac
lion   least
lunch   (letter)
little   (like)

baby - billfold
(bank)   binder
(bill)   (beast)
boa   blister

sandy - soccer
sunshine   (seat)
sock   (silly)
(saw)   socket

desk - dollhouse
(dip)   doctor
dusty   (dinner)
dough   donor

many - mind
mister   (maybe)
(map)   make
(meet)   (microphone)

tell - tollbooth
(test)   teacup
(today)   (temper)
(toad)   telephone

clip - cutlery
camera   (crush)
(cup)   (color)
clang   (crayon)

wagon - wobble
waddle   (wishbone)
well   would
worry   (whip)

In which book(s) would you look to find the following information? Mark each sentence according to the key.

D = dictionary   **A** = atlas   **T** = thesaurus   **E** = encyclopedia

A,E 1. How far is Africa from Asia?
T 2. What are synonyms for *good*?
D 3. How many meanings does *race* have?
E 4. Who was the thirteenth president of the U.S.?
D 5. Does the word *monkey* have an example sentence?
E 6. Write a report on Antarctica.
T 7. How many synonyms are there for *nice*?
D 8. Can the word *run* be both a noun and a verb?
A 9. What direction does I-75 run in the state of Ohio?
A,E 10. What did the first flag of our country look like?
T 11. Could *easy* be a synonym for *simple*?
A,E 12. On which continent is the Amazon River?
E 13. Write a report on solar energy.
D 14. How many syllables are in the word *tarantula*?
A,E 15. On which continent is India?

Page 36

English

Name _____

Match the common and proper nouns. Then write your own proper noun after each common noun.

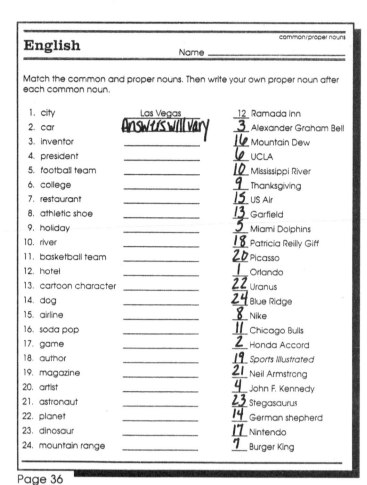

	Common noun	Your proper noun		Proper noun
1.	city	Las Vegas	12	Ramada Inn
2.	car	*Answers will vary*	3	Alexander Graham Bell
3.	inventor	_____	16	Mountain Dew
4.	president	_____	6	UCLA
5.	football team	_____	10	Mississippi River
6.	college	_____	9	Thanksgiving
7.	restaurant	_____	15	US Air
8.	athletic shoe	_____	13	Garfield
9.	holiday	_____	5	Miami Dolphins
10.	river	_____	18	Patricia Reilly Giff
11.	basketball team	_____	20	Picasso
12.	hotel	_____	1	Orlando
13.	cartoon character	_____	22	Uranus
14.	dog	_____	24	Blue Ridge
15.	airline	_____	8	Nike
16.	soda pop	_____	11	Chicago Bulls
17.	game	_____	2	Honda Accord
18.	author	_____	19	Sports Illustrated
19.	magazine	_____	21	Neil Armstrong
20.	artist	_____	4	John F. Kennedy
21.	astronaut	_____	23	Stegasaurus
22.	planet	_____	14	German shepherd
23.	dinosaur	_____	17	Nintendo
24.	mountain range	_____	7	Burger King

Page 37

English

Name _____

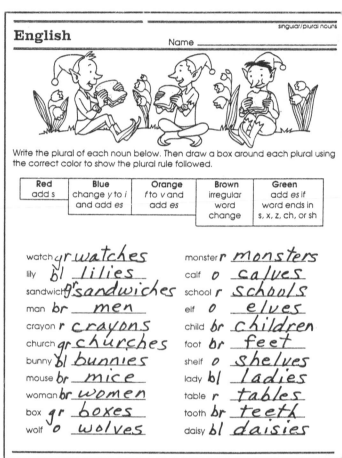

Write the plural of each noun below. Then draw a box around each plural using the correct color to show the plural rule followed.

Red	Blue	Orange	Brown	Green
add s	change *y* to *i* and add *es*	*f* to *v* and add *es*	irregular word change	add *es* if word ends in s, x, z, ch, or sh

watch *gr* watches
lily *bl* lilies
sandwich *gr* sandwiches
man *br* men
crayon *r* crayons
church *gr* churches
bunny *bl* bunnies
mouse *br* mice
woman *br* women
box *gr* boxes
wolf *o* wolves

monster *r* monsters
calf *o* calves
school *r* schools
elf *o* elves
child *br* children
foot *br* feet
shelf *o* shelves
lady *bl* ladies
table *r* tables
tooth *br* teeth
daisy *bl* daisies

Page 38

English

Name _____

In each football, write a pronoun that could take the place of the underlined words.

it	1. Football developed from soccer, although football players may throw the football or carry <u>the football</u>.
him	2. Lou Holtz's players at Notre Dame respect <u>Lou Holtz</u>.
our	3. <u>Chad and my</u> team won our division title.
us	4. The quarterback could pass the ball to <u>Brad and me</u>, since we were receivers.
its/their	5. The Michigan Wolverines won the Big Ten, <u>Michigan's</u> conference.
They	6. <u>The tackles</u> practiced and drilled four hours each day.
him	7. The coach sent in a play that the quarterback sent back to <u>the coach</u>.
his/her	8. The player's shoulder pads slipped off <u>the player's</u> shoulders.
it	9. The game was tied, so <u>the game</u> went into overtime.
them	10. The football officials met to discuss a decision one of <u>the officials</u> had made.
his/her their	11. If a player commits a penalty, <u>the player's</u> team is penalized by the loss of yards or a down.

Page 39

English

Name _____

For each picture, write two verbs to show actions the object could perform.

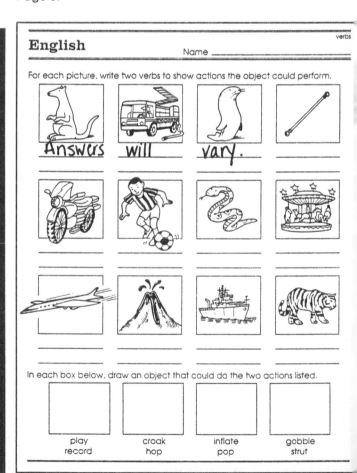

Answers will vary.

In each box below, draw an object that could do the two actions listed.

play record	croak hop	inflate pop	gobble strut

English

Name _____

Write two lines of conversation between the two characters given. Use quotation marks.

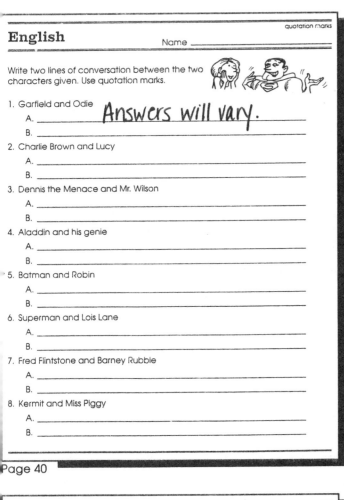

1. Garfield and Odie

    A. _____ Answers will vary. _____

    B. _____

2. Charlie Brown and Lucy

    A. _____

    B. _____

3. Dennis the Menace and Mr. Wilson

    A. _____

    B. _____

4. Aladdin and his genie

    A. _____

    B. _____

5. Batman and Robin

    A. _____

    B. _____

6. Superman and Lois Lane

    A. _____

    B. _____

7. Fred Flintstone and Barney Rubble

    A. _____

    B. _____

8. Kermit and Miss Piggy

    A. _____

    B. _____

English

Name _____

Write an example for each rule of capitalization.

Use capital letters on . . .

Answers will vary.

1. abbreviations _____
2. addresses _____
3. book titles _____
4. calendars _____
5. dates _____
6. the first word of a sentence _____
7. the first word of a quotation _____
8. friendly letters _____
9. initials _____
10. people's names _____
11. cities _____
12. companies _____
13. states _____
14. countries _____
15. a pronoun _____
16. stores _____
17. holidays _____
18. restaurants _____
19. cars _____
20. pet names _____
21. oceans _____
22. team names _____

English

Name _____

Write the abbreviation on the short crayon.

bldg. building	pp. pages	qt. quart
Mr. mister	jr. junior	Pres. president
p.o. post office	capt. captain	ave. avenue
F Fahrenheit	St. street	dept. department
Dr. doctor	mt. mountain	lb. pound
Oz. ounce	Sat. Saturday	cm centimeter
Feb. February	ft. foot	tbl. tablespoon
C Celsius	apt. apartment	Dec. December

English

Name _____

Write a friendly letter to your best friend describing the best summer vacation you ever had (real or imaginary). Then box each letter part in the color given in the mailbox.

(purple) _____
_____

Dear (red) _____

(orange) _____
_____
_____
_____
_____
_____
_____
_____
_____

body - orange
signature - blue
greeting - red
heading - purple
closing - green

(green)
(blue) _____

U.S. MAIL

© Instructional Fair, Inc.   113   IF8786 Fourth Grade in Review

English

adjectives

Name _____

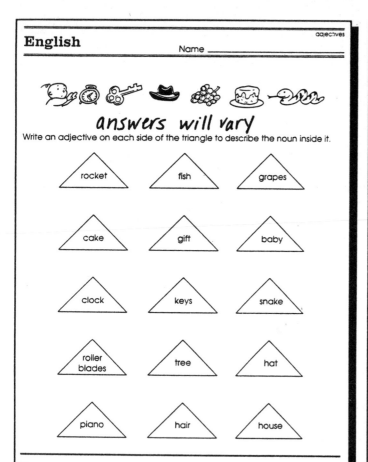

answers will vary

Write an adjective on each side of the triangle to describe the noun inside it.

- rocket
- fish
- grapes
- cake
- gift
- baby
- clock
- keys
- snake
- roller blades
- tree
- hat
- piano
- hair
- house

Page 44

English

adverbs

Name _____

Complete each sentence by writing an adverb that tells how, where, or when.

Answers will vary.

1. The baseball whizzed _____ past the batter.
   (how)
2. The crowd cheered _____.
   (how)
3. The shortstop threw _____ to first base.
   (how)
4. The players left their hotel _____.
   (when)
5. The American Airlines jet arrived _____.
   (when)
6. The Toronto Blue Jays traveled _____.
   (where)
7. Several opposing players wandered into the clubhouse _____.
   (when)
8. The outfielder ran _____ than the catcher.
   (how)
9. The team practiced _____ because of the rain.
   (where)
10. The umpire made the tough call _____.
    (how)
11. The team's manager argued the call _____.
    (how)
12. The rookie never batted _____.
    (how)
13. The stadium was built _____.
    (when)
14. Many of the fans departed _____ at the end of the ninth inning.
    (how)
15. The catcher threw the runner out _____.
    (how)
16. Baseball players exercise _____.
    (when)
17. We looked _____ when the ball was hit.
    (where)
18. The pitcher threw the ball _____.
    (where)

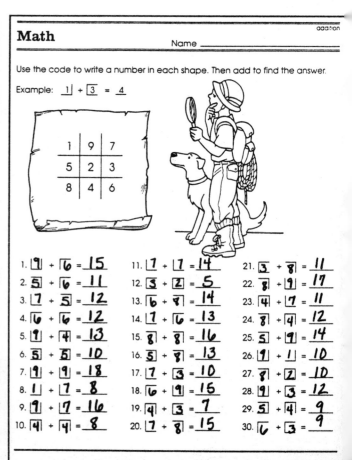

Page 45

English

parts of speech

Name _____

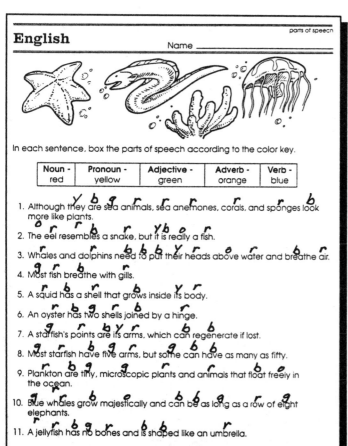

In each sentence, box the parts of speech according to the color key.

Noun - red	Pronoun - yellow	Adjective - green	Adverb - orange	Verb - blue

1. Although they are sea animals, sea anemones, corals, and sponges look more like plants.
2. The eel resembles a snake, but it is really a fish.
3. Whales and dolphins need to put their heads above water and breathe air.
4. Most fish breathe with gills.
5. A squid has a shell that grows inside its body.
6. An oyster has two shells joined by a hinge.
7. A starfish's points are its arms, which can regenerate if lost.
8. Most starfish have five arms, but some can have as many as fifty.
9. Plankton are tiny, microscopic plants and animals that float freely in the ocean.
10. Blue whales grow majestically and can be as long as a row of eight elephants.
11. A jellyfish has no bones and is shaped like an umbrella.

Page 46

Math

addition

Name _____

Use the code to write a number in each shape. Then add to find the answer.

Example: $\boxed{1} + \boxed{3} = \underline{4}$

1	9	7
5	2	3
8	4	6

1. $\boxed{9} + \boxed{6} = \underline{15}$
2. $\boxed{5} + \boxed{6} = \underline{11}$
3. $\boxed{7} + \boxed{5} = \underline{12}$
4. $\boxed{6} + \boxed{6} = \underline{12}$
5. $\boxed{9} + \boxed{4} = \underline{13}$
6. $\boxed{5} + \boxed{5} = \underline{10}$
7. $\boxed{9} + \boxed{9} = \underline{18}$
8. $\boxed{1} + \boxed{7} = \underline{8}$
9. $\boxed{9} + \boxed{7} = \underline{16}$
10. $\boxed{4} + \boxed{4} = \underline{8}$

11. $\boxed{7} + \boxed{7} = \underline{14}$
12. $\boxed{3} + \boxed{2} = \underline{5}$
13. $\boxed{6} + \boxed{7} = \underline{14}$
14. $\boxed{7} + \boxed{6} = \underline{13}$
15. $\boxed{8} + \boxed{8} = \underline{16}$
16. $\boxed{5} + \boxed{8} = \underline{13}$
17. $\boxed{7} + \boxed{3} = \underline{10}$
18. $\boxed{6} + \boxed{9} = \underline{15}$
19. $\boxed{4} + \boxed{3} = \underline{7}$
20. $\boxed{7} + \boxed{8} = \underline{15}$

21. $\boxed{3} + \boxed{8} = \underline{11}$
22. $\boxed{8} + \boxed{9} = \underline{17}$
23. $\boxed{4} + \boxed{7} = \underline{11}$
24. $\boxed{8} + \boxed{4} = \underline{12}$
25. $\boxed{5} + \boxed{9} = \underline{14}$
26. $\boxed{9} + \boxed{1} = \underline{10}$
27. $\boxed{8} + \boxed{2} = \underline{10}$
28. $\boxed{9} + \boxed{3} = \underline{12}$
29. $\boxed{5} + \boxed{4} = \underline{9}$
30. $\boxed{6} + \boxed{3} = \underline{9}$

Page 47

Math

Name _____

Write each problem using the code. Then find each answer.

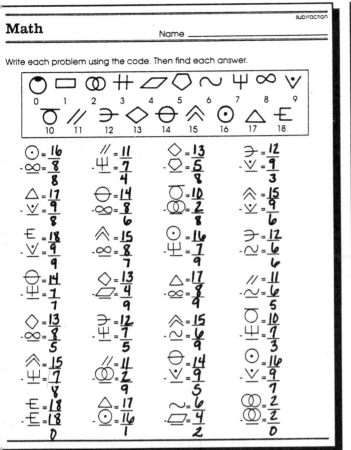

☉ = 16 - ∞ = 8 8	// = 11 - ⊣ = 7 4	◇ = 13 - ◇ = 5 8	∃ = 12 - ∨ = 9 3
△ = 17 - ∨ = 9 8	⊖ = 14 - ∞ = 8 6	○ = 10 - ◉ = 2 8	⩘ = 15 - ∨ = 9 6
E = 18 - ∨ = 9 9	⩘ = 15 - ∞ = 8 7	☉ = 16 - ⊣ = 7 9	∃ = 12 - ~ = 6 6
⊖ = 14 - ⊣ = 7 7	◇ = 13 - ◇ = 4 9	△ = 17 - ∞ = 8 9	// = 11 - ~ = 6 5
◇ = 13 - ∞ = 8 5	∃ = 12 - ⊣ = 7 5	⩘ = 15 - ~ = 6 9	⊢⊣ = 10 - ⊣ = 7 3
⩘ = 15 - ⊣ = 7 8	// = 11 - ◐ = 2 9	⊖ = 14 - ◐ = 9 5	☉ = 16 - ∨ = 9 7
E = 18 - E = 18 0	△ = 17 - ◉ = 16 1	~ = 6 - ◇ = 4 2	◐ = 2 - ◐ = 2 0

Page 48

Math

Name _____

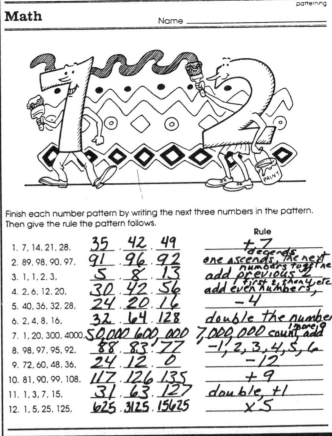

Finish each number pattern by writing the next three numbers in the pattern. Then give the rule the pattern follows.

				Rule
1. 7, 14, 21, 28,	35	42	49	+ 7
2. 89, 98, 90, 97,	91	96	92	depends, one ascends, the next the next numbers together
3. 1, 1, 2, 3,	5	8	13	add previous 2
4. 2, 6, 12, 20,	30	42	56	add even numbers, first 2, then 4, etc.
5. 40, 36, 32, 28,	24	20	16	− 4
6. 2, 4, 8, 16,	32	64	128	double the number
7. 1, 20, 300, 4000,	50,000	600,000	7,000,000	count, add 1 more 0
8. 98, 97, 95, 92,	88	83	77	−1, 2, 3, 4, 5, 6
9. 72, 60, 48, 36,	24	12	0	−12
10. 81, 90, 99, 108,	117	126	135	+ 9
11. 1, 3, 7, 15,	31	63	127	double, +1
12. 1, 5, 25, 125,	625	3125	15625	×5

Page 49

Math

Name _____

Show the place value of each underlined digit by outlining each placemat according to the color code.

ones - purple	one thousands - red	one millions - pink
tens - green	ten thousands - yellow	ten millions - brown
hundreds - orange	hundred thousands - blue	hundred millions - black

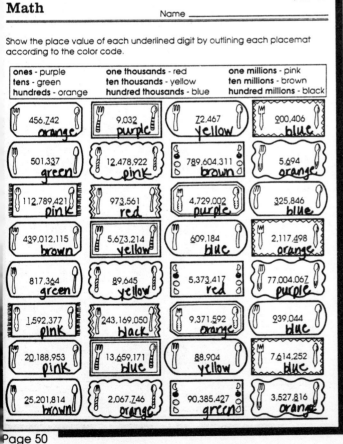

456,742 orange	9,032 purple	72,467 yellow	900,406 blue
501,337 green	12,478,922 pink	789,604,311 brown	5,694 orange
112,789,421 pink	973,561 red	4,729,002 purple	325,846 blue
439,012,115 brown	5,673,214 yellow	609,184 blue	2,117,498 orange
817,364 green	89,645 yellow	5,373,417 red	77,004,067 purple
1,592,377 pink	243,169,050 black	9,371,592 orange	239,044 blue
20,188,953 pink	13,659,171 blue	88,904 yellow	7,614,252 blue
25,201,814 brown	2,067,746 orange	90,385,427 green	3,527,816 orange

Page 50

Math

Name _____

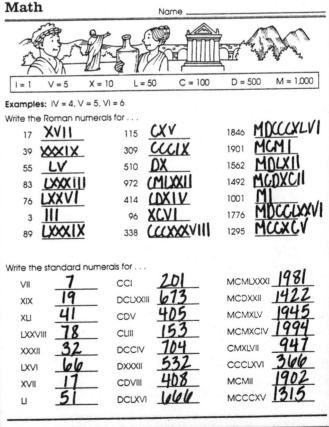

| I = 1 | V = 5 | X = 10 | L = 50 | C = 100 | D = 500 | M = 1,000 |

Examples: IV = 4, V = 5, VI = 6

Write the Roman numerals for . . .

17	XVII	115	CXV	1846	MDCCCXLVI
39	XXXIX	309	CCCIX	1901	MCMI
55	LV	510	DX	1562	MDLXII
83	LXXXIII	972	CMLXXII	1492	MCDXCII
76	LXXVI	414	CDXIV	1001	MI
3	III	96	XCVI	1776	MDCCLXXVI
89	LXXXIX	338	CCCXXXVIII	1295	MCCXCV

Write the standard numerals for . . .

VII	7	CCI	201	MCMLXXXI	1981
XIX	19	DCLXXIII	673	MCDXXII	1422
XLI	41	CDV	405	MCMXLV	1945
LXXVIII	78	CLIII	153	MCMXCIV	1994
XXXII	32	DCCIV	704	CMXLVII	947
LXVI	66	DXXXII	532	CCCLXVI	366
XVII	17	CDVIII	408	MCMII	1902
LI	51	DCLXVI	666	MCCCXV	1315

Page 51

Go through the maze by adding each number to the answer from the previous box.

Start
2,067
+ 1,000
3,067

+ 10,000
3067
13,067

+ 100
13067
13167

SWISS CHEESE SWAMP

+ 100
15177
15277

+ 1,000
14177
15177

+ 10
14167
14177

+ 1,000
13167
14167

GOUDA GULCH

+ 10,000
15277
25277

+ 10
25277
25287

+ 100
25287
25387

+ 10
25387
25397

+ 10
27407
27417

+ 1,000
26407
27407

+ 10
26397
26407

+ 1,000
25397
26397

MT. MOZZARELLA

+ 10,000
27417
37417

+ 10
37417
37427

+ 100
37427
37527

Page 52

Put an X on the box with the sign which should be used when comparing the pair of numbers. Write the letter from the X'd box on the matching numbered lines below to answer the riddle.

#	Left number	< box	> box	Right number
1.	164,982	N <	>X F	164,892
2.	27,493,171	C X <	> A	27,493,717
3.	13,562,439	R <	>X S	13,562,349
4.	60,871,956	M <	>X T	60,871,695
5.	34,742	C <	>X A	34,472
6.	19,584,578	D X <	> K	19,584,785
7.	746,361,294	N X <	> L	746,361,492
8.	600,100,001	B <	>X Y	600,010,001
9.	88,914,676	N X <	> T	88,914,767
10.	41,200,050	Y X <	> O	41,200,500
11.	841,762,145	D X <	> R	841,762,514
12.	27,181,426	N <	>X I	27,181,246
13.	38,226,943	P <	>X K	38,226,349
14.	80,000,001	O X <	> I	80,000,010
15.	500,146,271	S <	>X U	500,146,172
16.	15,836,504	N <	>X F	15,836,054
17.	20,673,746	R <	>X I	20,673,476

What do ducks call word meanings in their dictionaries?

D U C K Y   D A F F Y N I T I O N S
6 15 2 13 8   11 5 16 1 10 7 12 4 17 14 9 3

Page 53

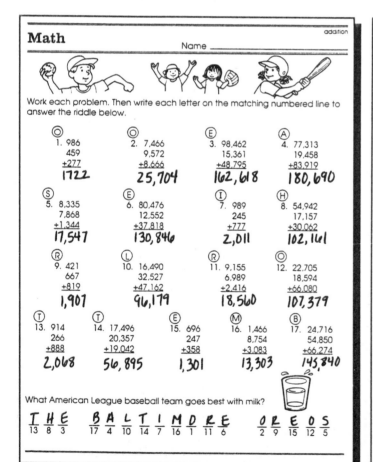

Work each problem. Then write each letter on the matching numbered line to answer the riddle below.

Ⓞ 1. 986 459 +277 = **1722**

Ⓞ 2. 7,466 9,572 +8,666 = **25,704**

Ⓔ 3. 98,462 15,361 +48,795 = **162,618**

Ⓐ 4. 77,313 19,458 +83,919 = **180,690**

Ⓢ 5. 8,335 7,868 +1,344 = **17,547**

Ⓔ 6. 80,476 12,552 +37,818 = **130,846**

Ⓘ 7. 989 245 +777 = **2,011**

Ⓗ 8. 54,942 17,157 +30,062 = **102,161**

Ⓡ 9. 421 667 +819 = **1,907**

Ⓛ 10. 16,490 32,527 +47,162 = **96,179**

Ⓡ 11. 9,155 6,989 +2,416 = **18,560**

Ⓞ 12. 22,705 18,594 +66,080 = **107,379**

Ⓣ 13. 914 266 +888 = **2,068**

Ⓣ 14. 17,496 20,357 +19,042 = **56,895**

Ⓔ 15. 696 247 +358 = **1,301**

Ⓜ 16. 1,466 8,754 +3,083 = **13,303**

Ⓑ 17. 24,716 54,850 +66,274 = **145,840**

What American League baseball team goes best with milk?

T H E   B A L T I M O R E   O R E O S
13 8 3   17 4 10 14 7 16 1 11 6   2 9 15 12 5

Page 54

Work each problem. If the answer is on a Bingo card, color the square. Draw a line through the winning row.

600 − 156 = **444**	2,146 − 1,098 = **1,048**	883 − 455 = **428**	6,114 − 3,762 = **2,352**	8,492 − 7,588 = **904**
411 − 77 = **334**	5,005 − 3,119 = **1,886**	708 − 499 = **209**	4,593 − 1,774 = **2,819**	3,051 − 1,662 = **1,389**
500 − 174 = **326**	9,384 − 5,745 = **3,639**	413 − 153 = **260**	2,001 − 966 = **1,035**	4,972 − 2,674 = **2,298**
624 − 335 = **289**	7,051 − 3,223 = **3,828**	904 − 713 = **191**	5,275 − 1,699 = **3,576**	3,231 − 869 = **2,362**
971 − 652 = **319**	5,047 − 2,736 = **2,311**	812 − 525 = **287**	6,711 − 4,472 = **2,239**	4,000 − 2,096 = **1904**

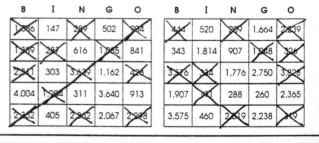

B	I	N	G	O
1,886	147	289	502	904
1,909	287	616	1,035	841
2,361	303	3,639	1,162	428
4,004	1,904	311	3,640	913
2,352	405	260	2,067	2,298

B	I	N	G	O
444	520	209	1,664	2,839
343	1,814	907	1,948	326
3,576	334	1,776	2,750	3,828
1,907	191	288	260	2,365
3,575	460	2,319	2,238	319

Page 55

Page 56

Name _____

Work each problem. Then lightly color the boxes blue whose answers have an "8" in them. This path should lead you to the island.

746 *b* +292 *l* **1038** *u* *c*	597 +366 **963**	943 +769 **1712**	848 +888 **1736**	357 +867 **1224**	677 +788 **1465**
499 *b* +799 *l* **1298** *u* *c*	385 *b* +496 *l* **881** *u* *c*	447 *b* +691 *l* **1138** *u* *c*	595 +377 **972**	201 +489 **690**	143 +798 **941**
355 +299 **654**	814 +296 **1110**	249 *b* +936 *l* **1185** *u* *c*	932 +384 **1316**	359 +367 **726**	484 +947 **1431**
649 +497 **1146**	390 +956 **1346**	479 *b* +369 *l* **848** *u* *c*	526 +577 **1103**	254 +996 **1250**	394 +777 **1171**
751 +179 **930**	947 +265 **1212**	542 *b* +939 *l* **1481** *u* *c*	963 *b* +872 *l* **1835** *u* *c*	307 +469 **776**	486 +293 **779**
875 +146 **1021**	436 +296 **732**	265 +171 **436**	596 *b* +274 *l* **870** *u* *e*	371 +639 **1010**	563 +199 **762**
195 +279 **474**	957 +285 **1242**	167 +448 **615**	194 *b* +588 *l* **782** *c*		

Addend Island

Page 57

Name _____

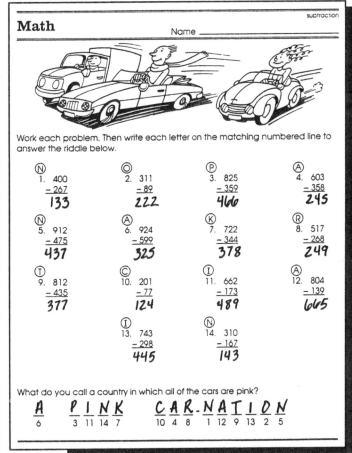

Work each problem. Then write each letter on the matching numbered line to answer the riddle below.

(N) 1. 400 − 267 = **133**

(O) 2. 311 − 89 = **222**

(P) 3. 825 − 359 = **466**

(A) 4. 603 − 358 = **245**

(N) 5. 912 − 475 = **437**

(A) 6. 924 − 599 = **325**

(K) 7. 722 − 344 = **378**

(R) 8. 517 − 268 = **249**

(T) 9. 812 − 435 = **377**

(C) 10. 201 − 77 = **124**

(I) 11. 662 − 173 = **489**

(A) 12. 804 − 139 = **665**

(I) 13. 743 − 298 = **445**

(N) 14. 310 − 167 = **143**

What do you call a country in which all of the cars are pink?

A   P I N K   C A R - N A T I O N
6   3 11 14 7   10 4 8   1 12 9 13 2 5

Page 58

Name _____

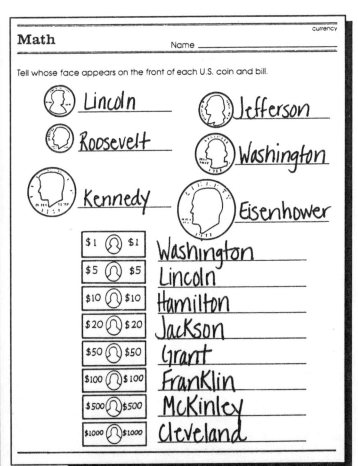

Watch the signs as you add and subtract these money problems.

$31.16 −17.47 **$13.69**	$84.12 +16.69 **$100.81**	$40.07 −26.49 **$13.58**	$57.45 +29.36 **$86.81**
$73.21 −46.09 **$27.12**	$53.29 +77.18 **$130.47**	$64.47 −19.56 **$44.91**	$81.51 +37.88 **$119.39**
$20.00 −6.43 **$13.57**	$37.14 +18.49 **$55.63**	$30.05 −9.98 **$20.07**	$57.69 +34.78 **$92.47**
$10.11 −5.16 **$4.95**	$86.55 +24.93 **$111.48**	$41.23 −27.88 **$13.35**	$25.95 +37.78 **$63.73**
$30.00 −6.46 **$23.54**	$71.86 +68.95 **$140.81**	$20.67 −4.98 **$15.69**	$39.99 +96.77 **$136.76**
$11.14 −6.35 **$4.79**	$56.49 +54.77 **$111.26**	$50.00 −39.77 **$10.23**	$57.66 +19.48 **$77.14**

Page 59

Name _____

Tell whose face appears on the front of each U.S. coin and bill.

Lincoln

Jefferson

Roosevelt

Washington

Kennedy

Eisenhower

$1	**Washington**
$5	**Lincoln**
$10	**Hamilton**
$20	**Jackson**
$50	**Grant**
$100	**Franklin**
$500	**McKinley**
$1000	**Cleveland**

Name _____

Draw the coins and/or bills you might receive as change in each situation.

You have . . .	Your purchase costs . . .	Your change is . . .
1. $10.00	$4.68	$5.32
2. $10.00	$6.98	$3.02
3. $15.00	$13.97	$1.03
4. $20.00	$10.45	$9.55
5. $25.00	$23.97	$1.03
6. $10.00	$5.67	$4.33
7. $5.00	$1.99	$3.01
8. $20.00	$14.62	$5.38
9. $3.00	$2.18	$.82
10. $10.00	$5.91	$4.09

Page 60

Name _____

Give the time to the exact minute.

6:51	10:12	8:03	12:27	7:23
1:16	3:32	9:48	2:12	11:09
5:24	4:54	8:56	12:49	6:29
7:18	3:01	9:26	1:41	2:07

Page 61

Name _____

Prince Pepperoni is busy baking at his Pizza Palace. Help him complete his baking schedule. The first one is done for you.

In the Oven	Baking Time	Out of the Oven
5:00	20 minutes	5:20
7:45	1½ hours	9:15
8:17	35 min	8:52
6:53	45 minutes	7:38
3:11	1 hour 15 minutes	4:26
7:12	48 min	8:00
3:47	25 minutes	4:12
9:08	46 min	9:54
10:05	1 hour 10 minutes	11:15
4:44	25 min	5:09
11:28	35 minutes	12:03

Page 62

Name _____

Below each box write a word using the numerical prefixes given. Then illustrate each word.

Answers will vary.

uni = 1 _____	bi = 2 _____
tri = 3 _____	quad = 4 _____
penta = 5 _____	kilo = 1000 _____
octo = 8 _____	deca = 10 _____

Page 63

Write the equation and product for each coded problem.

Example:
L x ∧ = 10
(5 x 2 = 10)

6 × 7 = **42**	5 × 5 = **25**	8 × 2 = **16**
9 × 3 = **27**	4 × 6 = **24**	9 × 4 = **36**
7 × 5 = **35**	7 × 7 = **49**	3 × 8 = **24**
9 × 9 = **81**	5 × 6 = **30**	7 × 4 = **28**
8 × 9 = **72**	8 × 8 = **64**	2 × 7 = **14**
5 × 8 = **40**	6 × 8 = **48**	4 × 5 = **20**
8 × 7 = **56**	3 × 3 = **9**	5 × 3 = **15**
6 × 6 = **36**	9 × 5 = **45**	4 × 4 = **16**
5 × 4 = **12**	7 × 6 = **42**	8 × 4 = **32**

Write each missing number.

24 ÷ 8 = **3**	16 ÷ **4** = 4	12 ÷ 2 = **6**	**36** ÷ 6 = 6
42 ÷ **6** = 7	**32** ÷ 4 = 8	18 ÷ 9 = **2**	20 ÷ **5** = 4
72 ÷ 9 = 8	12 ÷ 3 = **4**	64 ÷ **8** = 8	9 ÷ 3 = **3**
49 ÷ **7** = 7	**35** ÷ 5 = 7	48 ÷ **8** = 6	7 ÷ **1** = 7
30 ÷ 5 = **6**	**40** ÷ 5 = 8	**16** ÷ 2 = 8	24 ÷ 6 = **4**
81 ÷ 9 = 9	54 ÷ **9** = 6	18 ÷ 6 = **3**	**21** ÷ 7 = 3
27 ÷ 9 = **3**	28 ÷ **4** = 7	56 ÷ 7 = **8**	3 ÷ **1** = 3
48 ÷ 8 = 6	8 ÷ **4** = 2	**10** ÷ 5 = 2	**25** ÷ 5 = 5
36 ÷ **6** = 6	40 ÷ 5 = **8**	72 ÷ **8** = 9	12 ÷ **4** = 3
14 ÷ 7 = **2**	**49** ÷ 7 = 7	**9** ÷ 3 = 3	35 ÷ 7 = **5**
16 ÷ 4 = 4	32 ÷ **8** = 4	9 ÷ **1** = 9	**64** ÷ 8 = 8

Solve each problem.

3R3 5⟌18	**5R4** 6⟌34	**8R6** 8⟌70	**5R2** 8⟌42
6R1 9⟌55	**8R3** 5⟌43	**9R1** 2⟌19	**7R2** 9⟌65
6R6 7⟌48	**9R2** 3⟌29	**5R5** 7⟌40	**7R2** 4⟌30
7R4 6⟌46	**2R2** 9⟌20	**9R4** 6⟌58	**4R4** 8⟌36
3R3 4⟌15	**5R1** 3⟌16	**2R5** 8⟌21	**3R3** 7⟌24
4R1 2⟌9	**9R3** 5⟌48	**8R2** 4⟌34	**5R5** 9⟌50
6R2 3⟌20	**4R2** 9⟌38	**2R4** 7⟌18	**7R1** 6⟌43
5R4 9⟌49	**8R1** 2⟌17	**4R4** 6⟌28	**3R2** 3⟌11

Work a problem on your calculator. Write the answer. Then turn your calculator upside down and write the word to match each clue.

	Answer	Clue	Word
1. 10,252 – 2,538 =	**7714**	Raised land	**hill**
2. 1,777 × 4 =	**7108**	To heat water until it bubbles	**boil**
3. 2,864 + 2,799 =	**5663**	Go well with bacon	**eggs**
4. 253,867 × 2 =	**507734**	Salutations	**hellos**
5. 114,891 – 57,175 =	**57716**	Fish breathe through these	**gills**
6. 23,573 + 31,503 =	**55076**	A shiny finish	**gloss**
7. 1,401 × 4 =	**5604**	Big eaters	**hogs**
8. 11,543 × 5 =	**57715**	Window ledges	**sills**
9. 26,589 + 26,456 =	**53045**	Sock "mates"	**shoes**
10. 104,660 – 53,945 =	**50715**	Found on farms	**silos**
11. 94,154 × 4	**376616**	Laugh	**giggle**

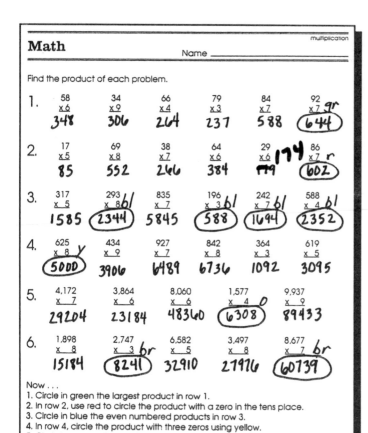

Math
multiplication

Name _____

Find the product of each problem.

1.
58 ×6 = 348   34 ×9 = 306   66 ×4 = 264   79 ×3 = 237   84 ×7 = 588   92 ×7 = (644) gr

2.
17 ×5 = 85   69 ×8 = 552   38 ×7 = 266   64 ×6 = 384   29 ×6 = 174 (79)   86 ×7 = (602) r

3.
317 ×5 = 1585   293 ×8 = (2344)   835 ×7 = 5845   196 ×3 = (588)   242 ×7 = (1694)   588 ×4 = (2352)

4.
625 ×8 = (5000) y   434 ×9 = 3906   927 ×7 = 6489   842 ×8 = 6736   364 ×3 = 1092   619 ×5 = 3095

5.
4,172 ×7 = 29204   3,864 ×6 = 23184   8,060 ×6 = 48360   1,577 ×4 = (6308) 0   9,937 ×9 = 89433

6.
1,898 ×8 = 15184   2,747 ×3 = (8241) br   6,582 ×5 = 32910   3,497 ×8 = 27976   8,677 ×7 = (60739) br

Now . . .
1. Circle in green the largest product in row 1.
2. In row 2, use red to circle the product with a zero in the tens place.
3. Circle in blue the even numbered products in row 3.
4. In row 4, circle the product with three zeros using yellow.
5. Circle in orange the smallest product in row 5.
6. In row 6, use brown to circle the largest and smallest products.

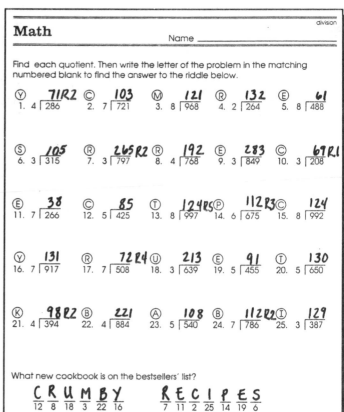

Math
division

Name _____

Find each quotient. Then write the letter of the problem in the matching numbered blank to find the answer to the riddle below.

(Y) 71R2   1. 4⟌286
(C) 103   2. 7⟌721
(M) 121   3. 8⟌968
(R) 132   4. 2⟌264
(E) 61   5. 8⟌488

(S) 105   6. 3⟌315
(R) 265R2   7. 3⟌797
(R) 192   8. 4⟌768
(E) 283   9. 3⟌849
(C) 69R1   10. 3⟌208

(E) 38   11. 7⟌266
(C) 85   12. 5⟌425
(T) 124R5   13. 8⟌997
(P) 112R3   14. 6⟌675
(C) 124   15. 8⟌992

(Y) 131   16. 7⟌917
(R) 72R4   17. 7⟌508
(U) 213   18. 3⟌639
(E) 91   19. 5⟌455
(T) 130   20. 5⟌650

(K) 98R2   21. 4⟌394
(B) 221   22. 4⟌884
(A) 108   23. 5⟌540
(B) 112R2   24. 7⟌786
(I) 129   25. 3⟌387

What new cookbook is on the bestsellers' list?

C R U M B Y   R E C I P E S
12 8 18 3 22 16   7 11 2 25 14 19 6

by B E T T Y   C R A C K E R
24 5 13 20 1   10 4 23 15 21 9 17

Page 69

Math
averaging

Name _____

The math teacher, Mrs. Numbers, needs your help in averaging math grades. Compute the average of each student.

Student	Grades					Average
1. Angie Addition	72	86	70	88	94	82
2. Cal Calculator	100	98	96	97	94	97
3. Dewey Decimal	84	72	83	76	80	79
4. Freddy Fraction	71	77	83	70	74	75
5. Mary Multiple	92	88	90	91	84	89
6. Perry Perimeter	70	80	73	75	77	75
7. Quincy Quotient	85	94	88	86	82	87
8. Randy Radius	65	70	68	71	66	68
9. Sarah Sphere	94	98	100	97	96	97
10. Teri Triangle	89	75	92	83	91	86

Page 70

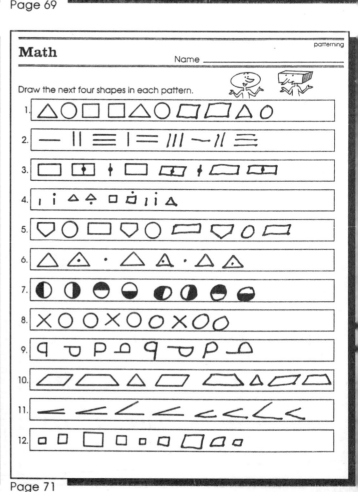

Math
patterning

Name _____

Draw the next four shapes in each pattern.

Page 71

Page 72

Math

Name _____

Write the correct term under each box.

Word Bank

pyramid	sphere	intersecting lines	line	pentagon
hexagon	cone	parallelogram	octagon	right angle
rectangle	cube	rectangular prism	triangle	parallel lines
				cylinder

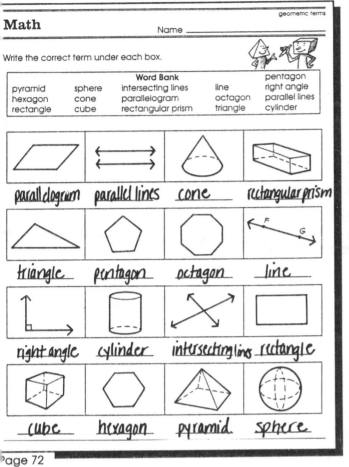

parallelogram   parallel lines   cone   rectangular prism

triangle   pentagon   octagon   line

right angle   cylinder   intersecting lines   rectangle

cube   hexagon   pyramid   sphere

Page 72

Page 73

Math

Name _____

Write the perimeter inside each shape.

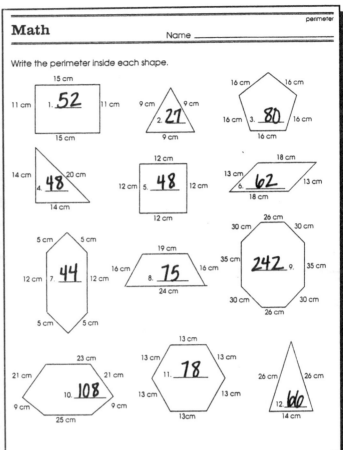

1. 52 (15 cm, 11 cm, 15 cm, 11 cm)
2. 27 (9 cm, 9 cm, 9 cm)
3. 80 (16 cm × 5)
4. 48 (14 cm, 20 cm, 14 cm)
5. 48 (12 cm, 12 cm, 12 cm, 12 cm)
6. 62 (18 cm, 13 cm, 18 cm, 13 cm)
7. 44 (5, 5, 12, 12, 5, 5)
8. 75 (19 cm, 16 cm, 24 cm, 16 cm)
9. 242 (26, 30, 35, 30, 26, 30, 35, 30)
10. 108 (23, 21, 9, 25, 9, 21)
11. 18 (13 cm × 6)
12. 66 (26 cm, 26 cm, 14 cm)

Page 73

Page 74

Math

Name _____

Multiply to find the area of each carpet. **Area = length x width**

24 ft. × 4 ft. A = **96** sq. ft.

13 ft. × 9 ft. A = **117** sq. ft.

6 ft. × 4 ft. A = **24** sq. ft

4 ft. × 9 ft. A = **36** sq. ft.

9 ft. × 9 ft. A = **81** sq. ft.

30 ft. × 3 ft. A = **90** sq. ft.

6 ft. × 17 ft. A = **102** sq. ft.

15 ft. × 8 ft. A = **120** sq. ft.

7 ft. × 16 ft. A = **112** sq. ft.

26 ft. × 2 ft. A = **52** sq. ft.

Page 74

Page 75

Math

Name _____

Find each product.

47 ×29	56 ×13	79 ×28	36 ×73	48 ×56	17 ×44
1363	728	2212	2628	2688	748

62 ×27	85 ×43	33 ×77	80 ×12	59 ×34	29 ×54
1674	3655	2541	960	2006	1566

57 ×68	96 ×27	88 ×54	27 ×54	88 ×67	93 ×26
3876	2592	4752	1458	5896	2418

842 ×16	665 ×28	748 ×34	893 ×56	667 ×45	854 ×18
13472	18620	25432	50008	30015	15372

394 ×76	746 ×17	377 ×28	858 ×33	972 ×75	631 ×14
29944	12682	10556	28314	72900	8834

291 ×26	179 ×66	814 ×27	485 ×89	349 ×58	723 ×44
7566	11814	21978	43165	20242	31812

Page 75

Math

Name _____

Complete each equivalent fraction.

1. $\frac{2}{4} = \frac{4}{8}$ 2. $\frac{3}{8} = \frac{6}{16}$ 3. $\frac{1}{3} = \frac{2}{6}$ 4. $\frac{3}{4} = \frac{12}{16}$

5. $\frac{1}{2} = \frac{6}{12}$ 6. $\frac{2}{7} = \frac{4}{14}$ 7. $\frac{3}{9} = \frac{1}{3}$ 8. $\frac{2}{5} = \frac{6}{15}$

9. $\frac{1}{6} = \frac{2}{12}$ 10. $\frac{3}{5} = \frac{9}{15}$ 11. $\frac{1}{6} = \frac{3}{2}$ 12. $\frac{3}{4} = \frac{9}{12}$

13. $\frac{4}{5} = \frac{8}{10}$ 14. $\frac{2}{6} = \frac{1}{3}$ 15. $\frac{2}{3} = \frac{6}{9}$ 16. $\frac{3}{5} = \frac{6}{10}$

Compare these fractions (< > =).

1. $\frac{4}{5} > \frac{2}{5}$ 2. $\frac{6}{10} > \frac{1}{10}$ 3. $\frac{2}{6} = \frac{1}{3}$

4. $\frac{1}{2} = \frac{2}{4}$ 5. $\frac{2}{8} < \frac{3}{4}$ 6. $\frac{1}{6} < \frac{4}{6}$

7. $\frac{2}{8} = \frac{1}{4}$ 8. $\frac{5}{8} > \frac{2}{8}$ 9. $\frac{2}{10} < \frac{4}{5}$

Write in the simplest terms.

1. $\frac{3}{6} = \frac{1}{2}$ 2. $\frac{4}{12} = \frac{1}{3}$ 3. $\frac{6}{9} = \frac{2}{3}$ 4. $\frac{4}{20} = \frac{1}{5}$

5. $\frac{6}{10} = \frac{3}{5}$ 6. $\frac{5}{15} = \frac{1}{3}$ 7. $\frac{2}{8} = \frac{1}{4}$ 8. $\frac{2}{10} = \frac{1}{5}$

9. $\frac{9}{12} = \frac{3}{4}$ 10. $\frac{8}{20} = \frac{2}{5}$ 11. $\frac{7}{14} = \frac{1}{2}$ 12. $\frac{9}{18} = \frac{1}{2}$

Page 76

Math

Name _____

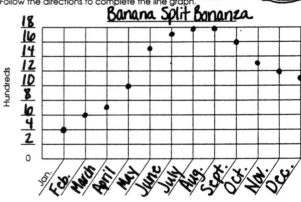

Follow the directions to complete the line graph.

Banana Split Bonanza

Hundreds: 18, 16, 14, 12, 10, 8, 6, 4, 2, 0

Jan., Feb., March, April, May, June, July, Aug., Sept., Oct., Nov., Dec.

1. Up the left side of the graph, number the Hundreds from 0 - 18, counting by twos.
2. On the diagonal lines, write each month beginning with January. Abbreviations may be used.
3. Above the graph, write the title **Banana Split Bonanza**.
4. Plot each point on the graph to show the number of banana splits sold each month.

Jan. – 4	May – 15	Sept. – 16
Feb. – 6	June – 17	Oct. – 13
March – 7	July – 18	Nov. – 12
April – 10	Aug. – 18	Dec. – 11

Page 77

Math

Name _____

The bar graph shows how much candy was sold in a candy drive. Use the graph to answer the questions.

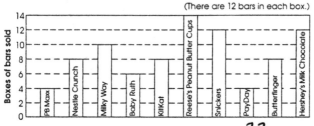

(There are 12 bars in each box.)

Boxes of bars sold: 14, 12, 10, 8, 6, 4, 2, 0

PB Maxx, Nestle Crunch, Milky Way, Baby Ruth, KitKat, Reese's Peanut Butter Cups, Snickers, PayDay, Butterfinger, Hershey's Milk Chocolate

1. How many boxes of Snickers and Milky Ways were sold? **22**
2. How many Hershey's bars were sold? **144**
3. How many more KitKat bars than PB Maxx bars were sold? **48**
4. Twelve boxes were sold of which candy bars? **Snickers and Hershey's milk chocolate**
5. How many Nestle Crunch and Baby Ruth bars were sold? **168**
6. How many more boxes of PayDays would have to be sold to equal the number of Hershey's boxes sold? **8**
7. How many packages of Reese's cups were sold? **168**
8. Less than 10 boxes were sold of which candy bars? **PB Max, Nestle Crunch, Baby Ruth, KitKat, PayDay, Butterfinger**
9. What is the difference in the amount of Milky Way and Butterfinger bars sold? **24**
10. What is the total number of boxes sold in the candy drive? **86**

*Challenge: What was the total number of candy bars sold? **1032**

Page 78

Math

Name _____

Fill in each box with +, –, x, or ÷ to make each math equation true.

1. 28 ÷ 4 × 3 = 21
2. 7 × 7 − 5 = 44
3. 6 ÷ 3 × 4 = 8
4. 72 ÷ 9 × 4 = 32
5. 3 + 3 × 6 = 36
6. 56 ÷ 7 × 4 = 32
7. 49 ÷ 7 × 6 = 42
8. 42 ÷ 6 + 8 = 15
9. 6 × 6 ÷ 6 = 6
10. 8 × 8 − 28 = 36
11. 2 × 7 + 14 = 28
12. 16 − 4 + 12 = 24

13. 35 ÷ 7 × 5 = 25
14. 11 − 4 − 1 = 6
15. 4 × 4 + 5 = 21
16. 6 − 4 × 7 = 14
17. 56 ÷ 7 × 3 = 24
18. 9 × 6 + 4 = 58
19. 5 × 4 − 3 = 17
20. 2 × 3 + 4 = 10
21. 24 ÷ 6 × 9 = 36
22. 12 ÷ 3 × 9 = 81
23. 24 ÷ 8 × 12 = 36
24. 72 ÷ 9 − 8 = 1

Page 79

Math

Name _____

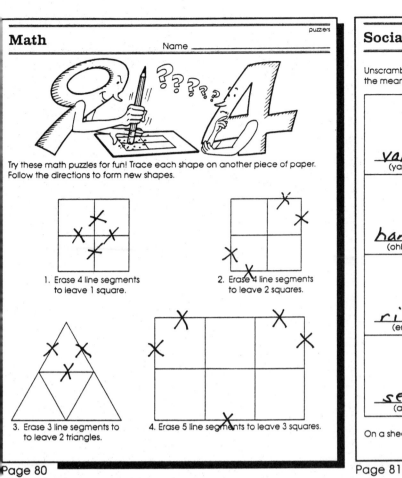

Try these math puzzles for fun! Trace each shape on another piece of paper.
Follow the directions to form new shapes.

1. Erase 4 line segments to leave 1 square.

2. Erase 4 line segments to leave 2 squares.

3. Erase 3 line segments to to leave 2 triangles.

4. Erase 5 line segments to leave 3 squares.

Page 80

Social Studies

Name _____

Unscramble and write each geographic term. Then draw a picture to illustrate
the meaning of each term.

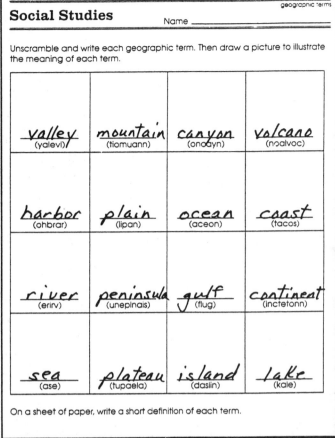

valley (yalevl)	mountain (tiomuann)	canyon (onoayn)	volcano (noalvoc)
harbor (ohbrar)	plain (lipan)	ocean (aceon)	coast (tacos)
river (erirv)	peninsula (unepinais)	gulf (flug)	continent (inctetonn)
sea (ase)	plateau (tupaela)	island (daslin)	lake (kale)

On a sheet of paper, write a short definition of each term.

Page 81

Social Studies

Name _____

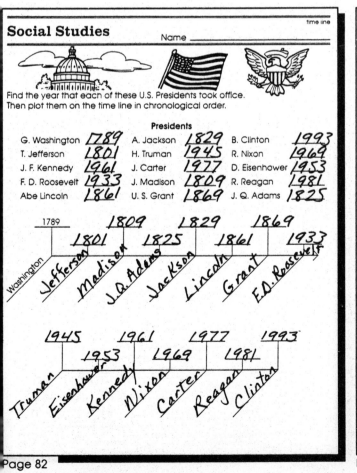

Find the year that each of these U.S. Presidents took office.
Then plot them on the time line in chronological order.

Presidents

G. Washington 1789	A. Jackson 1829	B. Clinton 1993
T. Jefferson 1801	H. Truman 1945	R. Nixon 1969
J. F. Kennedy 1961	J. Carter 1977	D. Eisenhower 1953
F. D. Roosevelt 1933	J. Madison 1809	R. Reagan 1981
Abe Lincoln 1861	U. S. Grant 1869	J. Q. Adams 1825

1789 1809 1829 1869
1801 1825 1861 1933
Washington Jefferson Madison J.Q. Adams Jackson Lincoln Grant F.D. Roosevelt

1945 1961 1977 1993
1953 1969 1981
Truman Eisenhower Kennedy Nixon Carter Reagan Clinton

Page 82

Social Studies

Name _____

Follow the directions to complete each globe.

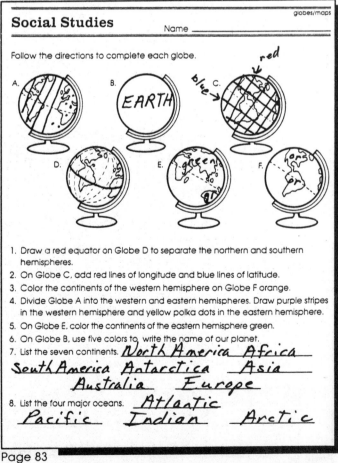

1. Draw a red equator on Globe D to separate the northern and southern hemispheres.
2. On Globe C, add red lines of longitude and blue lines of latitude.
3. Color the continents of the western hemisphere on Globe F orange.
4. Divide Globe A into the western and eastern hemispheres. Draw purple stripes in the western hemisphere and yellow polka dots in the eastern hemisphere.
5. On Globe E, color the continents of the eastern hemisphere green.
6. On Globe B, use five colors to write the name of our planet.
7. List the seven continents. North America Africa South America Antarctica Asia Australia Europe
8. List the four major oceans. Atlantic Pacific Indian Arctic

Page 83

Social Studies

Name _____

Follow the directions to complete the map.

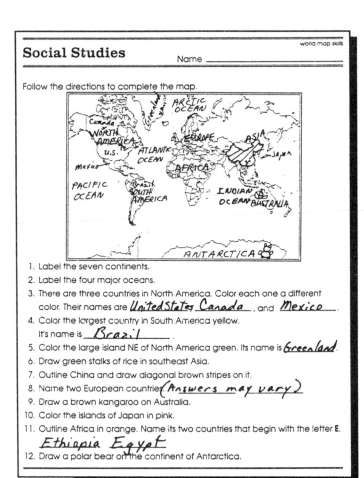

1. Label the seven continents.
2. Label the four major oceans.
3. There are three countries in North America. Color each one a different color. Their names are _United States_, _Canada_, and _Mexico_.
4. Color the largest country in South America yellow. It's name is _Brazil_.
5. Color the large island NE of North America green. Its name is _Greenland_.
6. Draw green stalks of rice in southeast Asia.
7. Outline China and draw diagonal brown stripes on it.
8. Name two European countries. _(Answers may vary)_
9. Draw a brown kangaroo on Australia.
10. Color the islands of Japan in pink.
11. Outline Africa in orange. Name its two countries that begin with the letter **E**. _Ethiopia Egypt_
12. Draw a polar bear on the continent of Antarctica.

Page 84

Social Studies

Name _____

Follow the directions to complete the map.

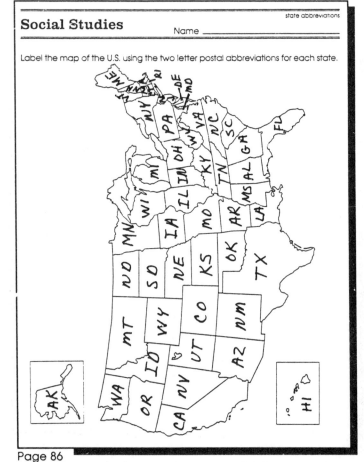

1. Trace the Mississippi River with blue.
2. Color the largest state with green polka dots. Its name is _Texas_
3. Color the smallest state yellow. Its name is _Rhode Island_
4. Outline all states beginning with **A** orange.
5. Add these brown symbols (∧∧) for the Rocky Mountains.
6. Label the five Great Lakes by writing the first letter of each name in blue. Name them. _Erie Michigan Superior Ontario Huron_
7. Put a green **2** on all states with two words in their names.
8. Put a red ★ on Washington, D.C., our nation's capital.
9. Outline the state where you live in black.
10. Put a red **V** on all states whose name starts with a vowel.
11. What country touches the U.S. on the north? _Canada_ south? _Mexico_
12. What ocean touches the east coast? _Atlantic_ west? _Pacific_
13. Put an orange **F** on the state that comes first in alphabetical order, and an orange **L** on the one that comes last. Name them. _Alabama Wyoming_
14. Draw a blue whale in the Gulf of Mexico.

Page 85

Social Studies

Name _____

Label the map of the U.S. using the two letter postal abbreviations for each state.

Page 86

Social Studies

Name _____

Complete the information about your state. _Answers will Vary._

1. Draw your state and write its name.

   State name _____

2. On your state label . . .
   ⊙ state capital
   • 4 major cities
     (blue) rivers
     (blue) lakes
     (brown) mountains

3. Your state nickname _____
4. Date of admission to the union _____
5. State motto _____
6. State bird _____
7. State flower _____
8. State tree _____
9. State song _____
10. Chief manufactured products _____
11. Natural resources _____
12. Interesting places to visit _____
    _____
    _____
13. States that border my state _____
14. Governor of my state _____
15. Draw your . . .

    | state bird | state flower | state flag |

Page 87

Social Studies

state capitals

Name _____

Match each state with its capital.

STATES

Alabama **15**   Indiana **46**   Nebraska **35**   South Carolina **33**
Alaska **4**   Iowa **23**   Nevada **25**   South Dakota **43**
Arizona **21**   Kansas **29**   New Hampshire **34**   Tennessee **1**
Arkansas **28**   Kentucky **32**   New Jersey **11**   Texas **11**
California **30**   Louisiana **22**   New Mexico **40**   Utah **39**
Colorado **31**   Maine **50**   New York **3**   Vermont **20**
Connecticut **47**   Maryland **48**   North Carolina **13**   Virginia **10**
Delaware **49**   Massachusetts **14**   North Dakota **27**   Washington **19**
Florida **45**   Michigan **2**   Ohio **8**   West Virginia **36**
Georgia **6**   Minnesota **26**   Oklahoma **42**   Wisconsin **44**
Hawaii **9**   Mississippi **12**   Oregon **24**   Wyoming **37**
Idaho **16**   Missouri **18**   Pennsylvania **7**
Illinois **5**   Montana **38**   Rhode Island **17**

CAPITALS

1. Nashville
2. Lansing
3. Albany
4. Juneau
5. Springfield
6. Atlanta
7. Harrisburg
8. Columbus
9. Honolulu
10. Richmond
11. Austin
12. Jackson
13. Raleigh
14. Boston
15. Montgomery
16. Boise
17. Providence
18. Jefferson City
19. Olympia
20. Montpelier
21. Phoenix
22. Baton Rouge
23. Des Moines
24. Salem
25. Carson City
26. St. Paul
27. Bismarck
28. Little Rock
29. Topeka
30. Sacramento
31. Denver
32. Frankfort
33. Columbia
34. Concord
35. Lincoln
36. Charleston
37. Cheyenne
38. Helena
39. Salt Lake City
40. Santa Fe
41. Trenton
42. Oklahoma City
43. Pierre
44. Madison
45. Tallahassee
46. Indianapolis
47. Hartford
48. Annapolis
49. Dover
50. Augusta

Which capitals do you think could have been named to honor presidents of the U.S.? **12, 18, 35, 44**

Social Studies

latitude/longitude

Name _____

Use the lines of latitude and longitude to identify and to plot countries.

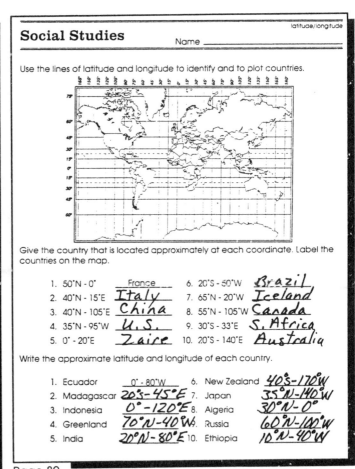

Give the country that is located approximately at each coordinate. Label the countries on the map.

1. 50°N - 0°   **France**
2. 40°N - 15°E   **Italy**
3. 40°N - 105°E   **China**
4. 35°N - 95°W   **U.S.**
5. 0° - 20°E   **Zaire**
6. 20°S - 50°W   **Brazil**
7. 65°N - 20°W   **Iceland**
8. 55°N - 105°W   **Canada**
9. 30°S - 33°E   **S. Africa**
10. 20°S - 140°E   **Australia**

Write the approximate latitude and longitude of each country.

1. Ecuador   **0° - 80°W**
2. Madagascar   **20°S - 45°E**
3. Indonesia   **0° - 120°E**
4. Greenland   **70°N - 40°W**
5. India   **20°N - 80°E**
6. New Zealand   **40°S - 170°W**
7. Japan   **35°N - 140°W**
8. Algeria   **30°N - 0°**
9. Russia   **60°N - 100°W**
10. Ethiopia   **10°N - 40°W**

Social Studies

Washington, D.C.

Name _____

Use the grid to answer the questions about Washington, D.C.

1. What famous residence is in B3? **White House**
2. The National Gallery of Art is in which grid? **D5**
3. Where is the U.S. Supreme Court? **D7**
4. What two things could you see at D1? **Lincoln Memorial + Vietnam Veterans Mem.**
5. What street runs between the House Offices in E6? **South Capitol St.**
6. The FBI is located in section **C4**
7. Laws are made in the Capitol at **D6**
8. What museum could you visit in D4? **Natural History**
9. Where is the Washington Monument located? **D3**
10. What could you find in section B6? **Union Station**
11. What street runs horizontally through C3? **Pennsylvania Ave.**
12. What government building is in section E4? **Department of Agri.**
13. Jefferson Drive runs between which two sections? **D4   D5**
14. What street runs diagonally through sections C1 and C2? **Virginia Ave**

Social Studies

famous Americans

Name _____

Use the Star-Spangled code to identify each famous American. Then match each person with his/her contribution to our country.

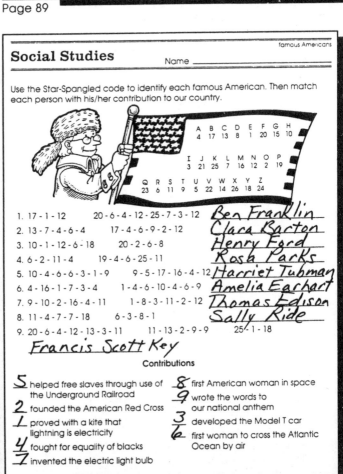

A	B	C	D	E	F	G	H
4	17	13	8	1	20	15	10

I	J	K	L	M	N	O	P
3	21	25	7	16	12	2	19

Q	R	S	T	U	V	W	X	Y	Z
23	6	5	22	14	26	18	24

1. 17 - 1 - 12   20 - 6 - 4 - 12 - 25 - 7 - 3 - 12   **Ben Franklin**
2. 13 - 7 - 4 - 6 - 4   17 - 4 - 6 - 9 - 2 - 12   **Clara Barton**
3. 10 - 1 - 12 - 6 - 18   20 - 2 - 6 - 8   **Henry Ford**
4. 6 - 2 - 11 - 4   19 - 4 - 6 - 25 - 11   **Rosa Parks**
5. 10 - 4 - 6 - 6 - 3 - 1 - 9   9 - 5 - 17 - 16 - 4 - 12   **Harriet Tubman**
6. 4 - 16 - 1 - 7 - 3 - 4   1 - 4 - 6 - 10 - 4 - 6 - 9   **Amelia Earhart**
7. 9 - 10 - 2 - 16 - 4 - 11   1 - 8 - 3 - 11 - 2 - 12   **Thomas Edison**
8. 11 - 4 - 7 - 7 - 18   6 - 3 - 8 - 1   **Sally Ride**
9. 20 - 6 - 4 - 12 - 13 - 3 - 11   11 - 13 - 2 - 9 - 9   25 - 1 - 18
   Francis Scott Key

Contributions

5 helped free slaves through use of the Underground Railroad
2 founded the American Red Cross
1 proved with a kite that lightning is electricity
4 fought for equality of blacks
7 invented the electric light bulb
8 first American woman in space
9 wrote the words to our national anthem
3 developed the Model T car
6 first woman to cross the Atlantic Ocean by air

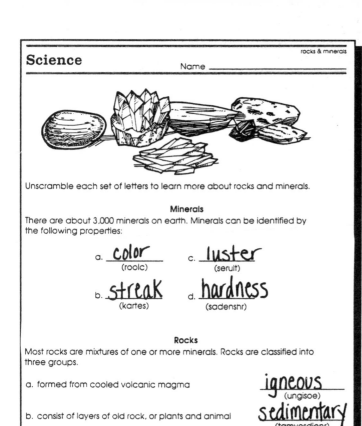

Unscramble each set of letters to learn more about rocks and minerals.

Minerals

There are about 3,000 minerals on earth. Minerals can be identified by the following properties:

a. **color**
(roolc)

c. **luster**
(serult)

b. **streak**
(kartes)

d. **hardness**
(sadensnr)

Rocks

Most rocks are mixtures of one or more minerals. Rocks are classified into three groups.

a. formed from cooled volcanic magma   **igneous**
(ungisoe)

b. consist of layers of old rock, or plants and animal   **sedimentary**
(tamyesdienr)

c. formed when minerals are changed by heat and pressure   **metamorphic**
(pamichrotem)

Write the name of each animal baby beside the correct animal. Write the letters from the boxes in the numbered blanks below to answer the riddle.

Word Bank				
chick	joey	cub	colt	gosling
eaglet	poult	fawn	cygnet	calf
foal	cub	kid	calf	

1. donkey **f o a l**
2. kangaroo **j o e y**
3. eagle **e a g l e**
4. turkey **p o u l t**
5. goose **g o s l i n g**
6. bear **c u b**
7. cattle **c a l f**
8. fox **c u b**
9. swan **c y g n e t**
10. goat **k i d**
11. deer **f a w n**
12. elephant **c a l f**
13. ostrich **c h i c k**

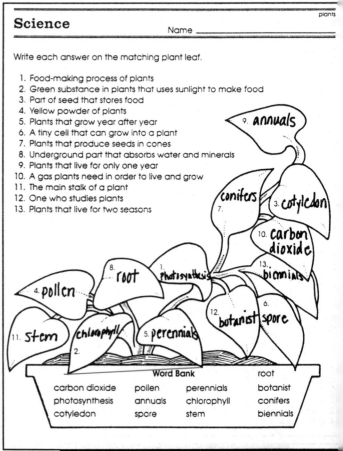

What duck has wings, feathers, and fangs?

$\underline{c}\ \underline{o}\ \underline{u}\ \underline{n}\ \underline{t}\quad \underline{d}\ \underline{r}\ \underline{a}\ \underline{k}\ \underline{e}\ \text{-}\ \underline{c}\ \underline{u}\ \underline{l}\ \underline{a}$
  6 1 8 11 3   10 7 13 2   9 4 5 12

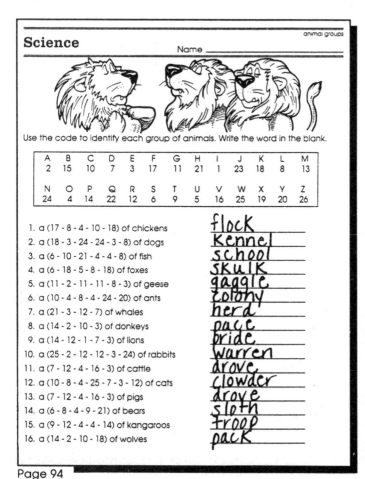

Use the code to identify each group of animals. Write the word in the blank.

A	B	C	D	E	F	G	H	I	J	K	L	M
2	15	10	7	3	17	11	21	1	23	18	8	13

N	O	P	Q	R	S	T	U	V	W	X	Y	Z
24	4	14	22	12	6	9	5	16	25	19	20	26

1. a (17 - 8 - 4 - 10 - 18) of chickens   **flock**
2. a (18 - 3 - 24 - 24 - 3 - 8) of dogs   **kennel**
3. a (6 - 10 - 21 - 4 - 4 - 8) of fish   **school**
4. a (6 - 18 - 5 - 8 - 18) of foxes   **skulk**
5. a (11 - 2 - 11 - 11 - 8 - 3) of geese   **gaggle**
6. a (10 - 4 - 8 - 4 - 24 - 20) of ants   **colony**
7. a (21 - 3 - 12 - 7) of whales   **herd**
8. a (14 - 2 - 10 - 3) of donkeys   **pace**
9. a (14 - 12 - 1 - 7 - 3) of lions   **pride**
10. a (25 - 2 - 12 - 12 - 3 - 24) of rabbits   **warren**
11. a (7 - 12 - 4 - 16 - 3) of cattle   **drove**
12. a (10 - 8 - 4 - 25 - 7 - 3 - 12) of cats   **clowder**
13. a (7 - 12 - 4 - 16 - 3) of pigs   **drove**
14. a (6 - 8 - 4 - 9 - 21) of bears   **sloth**
15. a (9 - 12 - 4 - 4 - 14) of kangaroos   **troop**
16. a (14 - 2 - 10 - 18) of wolves   **pack**

Write each answer on the matching plant leaf.

1. Food-making process of plants
2. Green substance in plants that uses sunlight to make food
3. Part of seed that stores food
4. Yellow powder of plants
5. Plants that grow year after year
6. A tiny cell that can grow into a plant
7. Plants that produce seeds in cones
8. Underground part that absorbs water and minerals
9. Plants that live for only one year
10. A gas plants need in order to live and grow
11. The main stalk of a plant
12. One who studies plants
13. Plants that live for two seasons

9. **annuals**
7. **conifers**
3. **cotyledon**
10. **carbon dioxide**
13. **biennials**
8. **root**
1. **photosynthesis**
4. **pollen**
12. **botanist**
6. **spore**
11. **stem**
2. **chlorophyll**
5. **perennials**

Word Bank			
carbon dioxide	pollen	perennials	root
photosynthesis	annuals	chlorophyll	botanist
cotyledon	spore	stem	conifers
			biennials

Science

Name _____

Use the picture, the clue, and the scrambled letters to write the name of each dinosaur.

Thunder lizard
apatosaurus
(rutapusaosa)

Three-horned
triceratops
(treposartci)

Large flier
pteranodon
(narotdepno)

Large thumb spike
iguanodon
(daugnoion)

Single row of plates
stegosaurus
(gaesrtusuos)

Huge plant-eater
brachiosaurus
(sarcbaruhoius)

Largest meat-eater
tyrannosaurus
(snotraysnurau)

Ostrich-like
ornithomimus
(hotmsronimui)

Covered with armored plates
ankylosaurus
(klsursanyoau)

Page 96

Science

Name _____

Label each diagram. Color as directed.

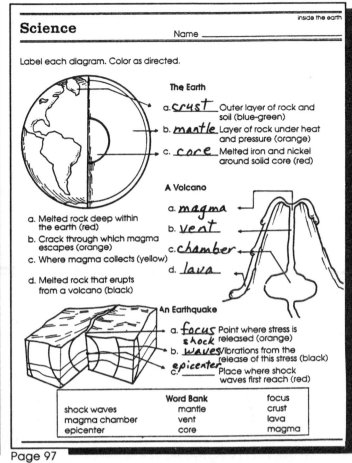

The Earth

a. **crust** Outer layer of rock and soil (blue-green)

b. **mantle** Layer of rock under heat and pressure (orange)

c. **core** Melted iron and nickel around solid core (red)

a. Melted rock deep within the earth (red)

b. Crack through which magma escapes (orange)

c. Where magma collects (yellow)

d. Melted rock that erupts from a volcano (black)

A Volcano

a. **magma**

b. **vent**

c. **chamber**

d. **lava**

An Earthquake

a. **focus** Point where stress is **shock** released (orange)

b. **waves** Vibrations from the release of this stress (black)

c. **epicenter** Place where shock waves first reach (red)

Word Bank		
shock waves	mantle	focus
magma chamber	vent	crust
epicenter	core	lava
		magma

Page 97

Science

Name _____

Complete the crossword puzzle.

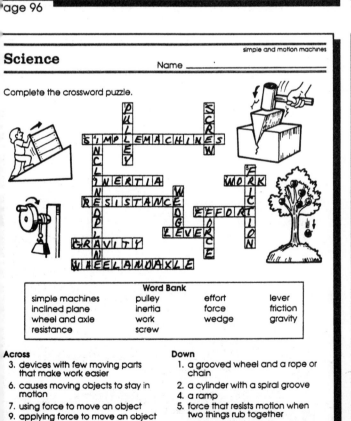

Word Bank			
simple machines	pulley	effort	lever
inclined plane	inertia	force	friction
wheel and axle	work	wedge	gravity
resistance	screw		

Across

3. devices with few moving parts that make work easier
6. causes moving objects to stay in motion
7. using force to move an object
9. applying force to move an object
10. the force used to do work
12. a bar used for prying
13. the pull toward earth's center
14. a handle and a stem

Down

1. a grooved wheel and a rope or chain
2. a cylinder with a spiral groove
4. a ramp
5. force that resists motion when two things rub together
8. triangular-shaped with an edge that tapers to a point
11. a push or a pull

Page 98

Science

Name _____

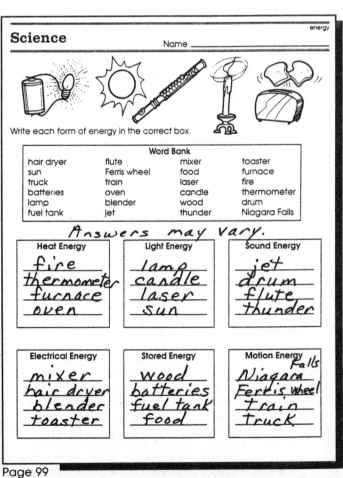

Write each form of energy in the correct box.

Word Bank			
hair dryer	flute	mixer	toaster
sun	Ferris wheel	food	furnace
truck	train	laser	fire
batteries	oven	candle	thermometer
lamp	blender	wood	drum
fuel tank	jet	thunder	Niagara Falls

Answers may vary.

Heat Energy
fire
thermometer
furnace
oven

Light Energy
lamp
candle
laser
sun

Sound Energy
jet
drum
flute
thunder

Electrical Energy
mixer
hair dryer
blender
toaster

Stored Energy
wood
batteries
fuel tank
food

Motion Energy
Niagara Falls
Ferris wheel
train
truck

Page 99

Write the answers in the blanks using the Word Banks.

Lunar Word Bank

| 1/6 | Apollo 11 | seas | lunar rover | lunar | craters | reflected | phases |

1. The moon's lowlands are called _seas_.
2. Many bowl-shaped _craters_ make up the moon's surface.
3. _Lunar_ refers to the moon.
4. ■◻◻◻◻◻◻◻ Symbols represent the _phases_ of the moon.
5. The moon has about _1/6_ the gravity of the earth.
6. The moon's light is _reflected_ from the sun.
7. _Apollo 11_ was the first U.S. spacecraft to land on the moon.
8. Astronauts traveled on the moon in a vehicle called a _lunar rover_

Solar Word Bank

| flare | million | sunspots | solar | 365 days | heat |
| star | helium | hydrogen | light | white dwarf | |

1. _Solar_ means relating to the sun.
2. The sun gives earth _heat_ and _light_.
3. The sun is really a _star_.
4. The sun is made mostly of the gases _helium_ and _hydrogen_.
5. It takes earth _365 days_ to orbit the sun.
6. Eventually, the sun will become a _white dwarf_.
7. Dark regions on the sun are called _sunspots_.
8. A _flare_ may result from the eruption of the sun's gases.
9. The earth is about 93 _million_ miles from the sun.

Write the name of the correct planet beside each clue.

Venus 1. The brightest planet in the sky
Mercury 2. Closest to the sun
Jupiter 3. Has a large area known as the *Great Red Spot*
Uranus 4. Is tipped over so far that it appears to roll
Pluto 5. The smallest planet
Jupiter 6. The largest planet
Earth 7. Has living organisms
Saturn 8. The second largest planet
Uranus 9. Has at least 11 rings and is seventh from the sun
Earth 10. Water makes up 71% of the planet's surface
Neptune 11. Eighth planet from the sun
Mars 12. Has huge volcanoes near its equator
Earth 13. 93 million miles from the sun
Venus 14. Once known as the *Evening Star*
Neptune 15. Contains a dark area known as the *Great Dark Spot*
Jupiter 16. Spins so fast it bulges at its equator
Mars 17. Two-thirds of the planet is reddish-brown

Draw and label the planets in the correct order from the sun.

Someday you may be interested in a career in science. Use the code box to match the job descriptions with the career.

A	B	C	D	E	F	G	H	I	J	K	L	M
3	26	11	7	4	23	12	14	2	22	16	8	18

N	O	P	Q	R	S	T	U	V	W	X	Y	Z
9	1	15	20	5	19	6	10	25	13	24	17	21

1. I study animal life.
zoologist
(21 - 1 - 1 - 8 - 1 - 12 - 2 - 19 - 6)

2. I am a space pilot.
astronaut
(3 - 19 - 6 - 5 - 1 - 9 - 3 - 10 - 6)

3. Using our natural resources properly is my main concern.
conservationist
(11 - 1 - 9 - 19 - 4 - 5 - 25 - 3 - 6 - 2 - 1 - 9 - 2 - 19 - 6)

4. I design circuitry.
electrical engineer
(4 - 8 - 4 - 11 - 6 - 5 - 2 - 11 - 3 - 8   4 - 9 - 12 - 2 - 9 - 4 - 4 - 5)

5. I study plant life.
botanist
(26 - 1 - 6 - 3 - 9 - 2 - 19 - 6)

6. The universe is my area of study.
astronomer
(3 - 19 - 6 - 5 - 1 - 9 - 1 - 18 - 4 - 5)

7. I study the origin of human beings.
anthropologist
(3 - 9 - 6 - 14 - 5 - 1 - 15 - 1 - 8 - 1 - 12 - 2 - 19 - 6)

8. The recovery and study of the remains of a past culture is my job.
archaeologist
(3 - 5 - 11 - 14 - 3 - 4 - 1 - 8 - 1 - 12 - 2 - 19 - 6)

9. I mix different kinds of matter to make new materials.
chemical engineer
(11 - 14 - 4 - 18 - 2 - 11 - 3 - 8   4 - 9 - 12 - 2 - 9 - 4 - 4 - 5)

10. I study and forecast weather.
meteorologist
(18 - 4 - 6 - 4 - 1 - 5 - 1 - 8 - 1 - 12 - 2 - 19 - 6)

11. Rocks and minerals are my interests.
geologist
(12 - 4 - 1 - 8 - 1 - 12 - 2 - 19 - 6)

12. I design machines using heat and power.
mechanical engineer
(18 - 4 - 11 - 14 - 3 - 9 - 2 - 11 - 3 - 8   4 - 9 - 12 - 2 - 9 - 4 - 4 - 5)

About the Book

This is a great activity book which can be used in the spring for review, or in the summer or fall to brush up on skills from the previous year. The author has used a variety of activities which every child will enjoy while reviewing Reading, Creative Writing, Critical Thinking, English, Math, Social Studies, and Science.

Credits

Author: Jan Kennedy
Artist: Catherine Yuh
Project Director/Editor: Sue Sutton
Editors: Alyson Kieda,
            Mary Ann Valenti Boyer
Production: Jeff Waibel
* **Cover Photo:** Frank Pieroni

* Cover photo taken of the Rounds School in Rockford, MI. Permission to use given by the Rockford Rotary Club.